HOW I MADE IT
(Through the fire without a burn on me)

I'M A SURVIVOR

Tanya D Mills-Forbes September 14th 2008 this book was written to help Inspire everyone who opens it, and really read with understanding where I'm the writer am coming from with real life experiences.

Ephesians 6:10- 24

Acknowledgments

I would like to first of all give all praise to my king my Lord and Savior Jesus Christ for even giving me a chance when I wouldn't give myself a chance for choosing me to such a responsibility as this without Jesus Christ none of this would be possible, secondly I would like to acknowledge my blessed children who I know loves me no matter what for understanding me in my hard to understand moments, for accepting me for who I am for praying for me, in my most sickest times thank you Marcus, Tanasia, Marquies, and Victoria for the love the faith in me to be who God called me to be. For putting up with me, in my happy times, my Angry times my I was wrong times for trusting me in my I'm not sure times. I love all of you, and without each of you, I wouldn't have made it this far I want you guys to know I appreciate every last one of your different spirits. I love you all with all of my heart please for me live your life for Jesus Christ. Thirdly I would like to thank all my family, friends, and friend enemies who have been in my corner to help me in my life. Thank you! I would like to acknowledge all the mighty men, and women of God who have prayed for me, inspired me and also believed God in me some are still here and well, some are gone home to be with the Creator thank you God bless you all. Philippians 4:13 I can do all things through Christ who strengthens me. Remember don't let people, life experiences, death, pain, and the unexpected, dictate to you who you are. Don't settle for poverty. God has the first and the last word on your life. Isaiah 54:17 no weapon formed against you shall prosper and every tongue which Rises against you in judgement you shall condemn. As the old saying goes you better know what you want because you might get it, and you've got to accept it whether you succeed or whether you encounter adversity you always have to believe in your worth as a person. That's what counts. Remarks at a success seminar in Portland Oregon February 6th, 2001.

Contents:

1. THE RUNAWAY GIRL(MOM DAD &THE FAMILY)

2. THEY SAID I WAS HOPELESS(MOM DAD & THE FAMILY)

3. STREET LIFE(IN & OUT OF JAIL, HOMELESSNES, DRUGS ETC...)

4. SINGLE MOTHER(THE SPERM DONOR, THE CHILDREN, THE FATHER)

5. TIME TO CHANGE(DEATH OF CLOSE LOVED ONES & FRIENDS)

6. THE MARRIED LIFE(ME & MY HUSBAND)

7. SWIM OR DROWN(TIRED OF THE STRUGGLING)

8. HOLDING ON (LETTING GO & LETTING GOD)

9. RELIGION(MY LIFE, MY FAITH, MY BELIEVE DEALING WITH WITCHES WARLOCKS, & THE UNKNOWN)

I'M A SURVIVOR(HOW I MADE IT THIS FAR WITH MY GOD)

HOW I MADE IT... THROUGH THE FIRE WITHOUT A BURN ON ME!!

I'M A SURVIVOR

HOW I MADE IT...

CHAPTER ONE

The Runaway Girl.

The runaway girl.

     I was born in 1974 in Hempstead Long Island East Meadow hospital to the late mother Brenda L Mills my mother had six children at the time I was her seventh, I remember growing up under my older siblings where they would take turns doing whatever I was in need of, whether it was fixing my food, to giving me a bath or doing my hair. It was only two I can see clear of their faces helping me, I will just say Josh & Jill both of their names started with J's.

I remember mom would yell and make them attend to me whether they felt like it or not they were doing what I was in need of at all times. Now due to me being in the Foster family with them from six months to four years old Me, Jill, and Josh had to stay with a foster family. Then upon the separation they let me stay with my big sister due to her being the oldest girl at the time.

We had lived with the family in Amityville NY until the foster family decided to return us back to our mother. The Foster family were Jehovah Witnesses.

The family had four children of their own when they added me, and my two siblings to that family it was why I only remembered my two siblings always taken care of me Josh and Jill was the two I would see all the time the Foster family always had us in church at the Kingdom Hall. Once we were placed back with our mother, life began to shift really fast.

We moved from New York in 1981 I remember we moved to Summit Hills and Silver Spring Maryland in 1981. We lived there for some years. I went to Rosemary Hills Elementary School, Westland junior high school, and Albert Einstein High School in which I didn't finish. I went to the 10th grade and dropped out, I stopped going as my life began to change rapidly spiritually, and naturally due to some things I was unaware of at the time I was ten years old.

In 1983 My Life was shifted seriously due to my dad putting witchcraft on me, to use me as one of his sacrifices to gain worldly riches to have control over my life. By the time I'm 12 years old I was fully possessed with demons, and I didn't know it. I thought I was normal, and okay. In the year of 1986, I was 12 years old this is where the runaway girl came alive.

I was 12 years old when the streets started being my best friend at this time in my life I was raising my younger sisters, and brothers the five that are younger than me became my own children from, dressing them, cooking for them, cleaning and styling they hair, and having them with me every time I left out the door. If you see me, you seen one of my siblings with me. Now granted mom taught me how to cook at nine years old, so when her, and dad were always at work someone had to hold the house down.

So, me being the oldest at that time it fell on me. If Mom and Dad would come home, and the choirs weren't done, the kids had dinner, dishes washed, and put away, bathroom clean, floors vacuumed, and everything in order, that was my head on the chopping block, and beatings would be my portion. Now mind you I couldn't talk on the phone at home with my friends, I had no outside social life while in the house, so every chance I got to sneak on the phone I will do it.

Which will put me back on the time they were supposed to come home and me having everything done, and sleep or playing sleep in the bed. Some nights if I wasn't being woken up to a belt or a slap in the face for the stove not being clean, or the dishes not put away, or the bathroom not cleaned. Don't forget the floor if it hadn't been vacuumed that was me getting the beatdown.

Having a lot of responsibilities at a young age, made me act out in school, along with the torment of Witchcraft that was also taken place on me. At my unawareness being innocent in the spirit, and natural. Unaware of the actions, and feelings that came with this torment. School was the only place I felt like I could do me, and not have any kids on my back, and not being in jail in my mind. I can remember Elementary was good. I love going to school to see my friends and teachers. Middle School was a little different.

At this time of my life I'm going through puberty, and I'm learning how to stay cute, and fly in my Big Brother's clothes. Late at night I will sneak and take his pants, and shirts so that I can have name brand clothes for school the next day. I also remember the incest between me and him, another demonic activity that was taking place in my parent's house that was just energy from the dark side to having me act out of control.

In school I was a ringleader around my friends. I always made sure I was seen and heard. If I didn't like you, I would be mean to you. In class I wouldn't do my own class work, I would cheat on my class work and get the homework from someone in class who did it. The teacher would be in front of the class writing on the chalkboard, and I'm throwing things at my classmates behind the teachers back, Paper spitballs, balled up paper, paperclips you name it. I was doing it just to get a laugh, and respect from my classmates. I was a bully, and I ran with some of the best of the baddiest girls in the school. This would go on until I was put out of class with detention or suspension. High School wasn't so fun, still I'm wearing everybody else's clothes but my own. Due to my parents not taking me shopping with the latest trends.

So, I will find my brothers, cousins, and Friends closet to get my next fit for the next day of school. Peer pressure was real, I had to keep up with my image as this fly girl, bad girl, that I was growing into automatically. I had to be on point, so that no one would talk about me, and make me feel less than who I was growing to be. I had to uphold my image of being like that and running the show.

This High School is where the rubber meets the road. Girls were ready by now to stand up for themselves, and I found myself in more and more fights. From the girls locker room to the bus stop getting off the bus. I lost some fights, and I won some fights. Finding myself in more and more drama back-to-back.

My reputation at school was very important to me, I was trying my best to be a good leader of those my peers who like me, while I was on a time limit of doing so. At the end of the day I had to go back home to what I looked at as jail, no phone, no chill time, no friend time, just time to clean, cook and watch the kids.

All of this went on the whole 10th grade school year I got in my mind to start to run away from home. I will spend the night over friends' houses. My friends would do as much as they could in their power to help me in any kind of way.

When I would ask for their help, by sleeping in their homes, getting sneaked into their homes, sleeping under their beds, eating their families food, taking showers, and I'm doing my hair in their homes. Of, course the parents didn't want me nowhere around their kids, but we were friends so they would take the risk for me, most of the time. Until that came to an end. I will get myself together in their homes without the family knowing I was even in there. I noticed as I ran away from home my demonic activity started getting bigger.

I began stealing cars, hanging on street corners, and selling drugs. At this time in my life I'm meeting new friends, and my desire to be on my own was going so fast. I didn't have money unless I made it by selling drugs, when I didn't have any drugs to sell, I would sell my body. Prostitution is now on me like running water. I'm having more than one hustle in me for the day.

As I approached the night I had to find where I was going to sleep for that night, all within the day. I would have to plan my day early in the morning. It was a daily lifestyle for me until I found myself in the Receiving Home, the jail for juveniles. This is where I got my first Godmother. Ms.

Barbra was one of the councilors who managed the girls side of the unit. G unit that was. She saw the light in me, took to my likeness, and began taking care of me. When she noticed I had no family visits, and no proper hygiene products for myself. Thank God for her, she would sneak them in there for me. Just like the Popeyes Chicken amongst other things I needed. It's a Holding Center for troubled bad children. Basically, a baby jail for the young adults. Well I found myself getting locked up for a stolen car in 1991, and also found out in this place that I was pregnant with my first son.

At this time, I didn't want a baby. It would slow my lifestyle down, from going place to place whenever I will get the mind to, working the streets. Once I got settled into this Receiving Home place, they took me to the nurse area where they did a physical on me. They took my blood, it was then I'm told you're pregnant, and because you're underage we must call a meeting with your parents.

I told the lady not to call my parents, and that I was going to have an abortion the nurse told me it's not up to me that my parents had to sign for me if they wanted me to get rid of the child. I wanted an abortion because I had nowhere to live once, I was to be released from this place, and I refused to go back home with my parents. I thought my parents would love to participate for me by signing the abortion papers for me. The counselor called them in for the meeting they came and didn't agree on signing the abortion papers.

In 7 months, I will give birth to my son. I went back to court, and the judge ordered for me to go back to my parent's house. A place I didn't really want to go. I had nowhere to go so my choices were few, and I found myself back into my parent's home. At this time my parents lived in Wheaton Maryland on Floral street. When it's time for me to deliver my son, my parents were nowhere in the area on purpose. They were in Atlantic City at Dover Downs. Looking to win some money, so I had no choice but to call my Aunt Janice to take me to the hospital to have this son of mine. She took me, and hours later my son was born.

Now at this time I'm ignorant of the things of God, as well as the things of the spirit realm and the operations of witchcraft. With Aunt Janice being the one in the delivery room with me, I thought all would be well unfortunately it wasn't; it was a plot in a plan being played out since 1983 when her, and my father began to experiment on me in the spirit with their witchcraft. Aunt Janice was in the room with me, and my child. She was meditating, initiating, and praying on my son and myself in spiritual witchcraft ways.

I was ignorant of witchcraft at the time. Having my son was a very painful experience for the first time. I was hoping to go back home, and things would be better and changed. I wouldn't mind being home, but nothing changed. Now I have my son, and my spirit is not at peace with my so-called family. I always felt like a stranger or slave in my parent's home. After my body healed, from having the baby.

I began to work in different places. The person who I thought was my child's father, wasn't the father. So, I'm raising my son by myself with the help of my mother, and sisters, at this time. I was working and between my mom, sisters, and babysitter they would help watch my son for me. I would get a job, but none will make me permanent. Jobs will come and go for a while, until I get tired of the runaround, and the jobs play out. My mind went straight to the streets. One place I found a peace of mind, and I will be happy. I can make me, and my son some real money real fast.

The runaway girl is back at her plan. Okay now I got to make a deal with my mom without my dad knowing about it. Without me realizing it this idea really worked out between Mom and me. I asked my mom if she can find a babysitter for my son, and that I will pay for his childcare, his food, and his clothes. Mom found Miss Beatrice to take care of my son, while she went to work, and I was doing my thing on the streets.

Miss Beatrice was watching my son up until the time I began to see things changing with my mom, without her communicating with me like we used to. I will pay my mom money to give the babysitter for pampers, and clothes for my son. Mind you once I made up my mind to do the streets. I ask my parents if my son can stay in their home, and I would pay for him to stay there. It was all a go.

Dad agreed when mom brought it to his attention for a little while at this time my sister's Bridget and Gigi are helping Mom in the home to take care of my son. I'm back into the streets now, so at this time I trusted my family to take good care of my son while I was away. This is the time the demons begin to have fun with my son in the same house on Floral Street, where incest was taking place right under mom's nose.

My son went through a tough time in this house but it's not up to me to tell his story. He was there until 4 years old. My Son staying with them, went on until one night the Lord came to me and said the streets or your son? I responded to the voice of the Lord my son. The next day the Lord told me to go and get my son. This had come to my mind early that day.

I sold all my drugs off, and my son was my next mission. I went straight to Wheaton Maryland, to get my son. By the time I arrived to get my son from taking that long bus ride from northwest DC to Wheaton, Maryland, where he had been living. Nighttime has come, I went to knock on the door of 3404 Floral Street, to see my mom, and pay her for the week, also to let her know my son was coming with me.

Well that's not what happened, I knocked on the door in fear. Instantly I felt the spirit of fear come over me, Because I knew my dad was home, and this meant problems. I knew it was going to be a problem, with me knocking on the door this time of the night. Dad and Mom had already come home from work, but I didn't care. I heard the Lord tell me to go and get my son.

I knocked on the door, and Dad answered the door. I let him know I was there to take my son with me. He shut the door in my face and refused to bring my child to me. I went two houses down to my grandmother's house at the time to get my cousin Rachel. I asked her if she could go with me to the police station, so they could make my parents give me back my son. By now my Dad is on the phone with my grandmother telling her not to let me in her house, and not to talk to me along with a lot of other rude, and nasty things.

All to keep my Grandma, and Cousin Rachel from listening to my side of the story. My Cousin Racheal gets out of the house and calls us a cab to the police station. I paid for the cab, mom and dad with my son drove to the police station. God is so good once we all went into the room together to talk about me coming to take my son back with me, the police made my parents release my son to me right there. If I had waited any longer my dad was going to make mom get custody, and a public assistance check for my son, while he was staying in their home.

The runaway girl, God is so good even in the midst of my life being the way it was. Doing whatever I had to do to survive, I could still hear the voice of the Lord, and Holy Spirit. In spite of all the obstacles, and torment from the witchcraft spirits.

That morning, and night If I didn't listen to the voice of the Holy Spirit I wouldn't have or known my son to this day. The runaway girl that's what I was, running from house to house pillow to pole. I found the family of one of my clients who was on drugs at the time. I had no clue the son, and the mother was family. This family stuck with me very closely, as me, and Ms.Cathy's son began to be boyfriend and girlfriend. I happened to stumble on this one. One day I went into the building on Clifton Street, NW to make a sale.

After that my Spirit led me in the hallway of about 5 young dudes in a circle. One of the guys I knew. I looked at all of them, and the Lord told me to pull Steve, and tell him to hook me up with Darell.

One of the young guys in this hallway. The Lord told me that this young boy was going to be my place to stay. His mom, and I had already known each other because we had business together, drug business that was. God bless them for accepting me, and my son when we didn't have anywhere else to go.

Their home became my home until I didn't no longer needed them anymore, the Kirkland family. They already had their own family, the mother, the daughter, and the grandkids.

All in the same house. True love it was, and no evil spirits controlling the house or you. This was a clean by spirit, and dirty by eyesight type of house. Oh well it was a new place to call home for me, and my son. The mom was one of my best customers. She ended up being someone very dear and loving in my heart. I loved this lady. The son became my boyfriend, fighter, and hater, and the rest fell into place like dominoes.

The runaway girl, now from Wheaton Maryland to Northwest Washington, DC this was great for me at the time due to everything at hands reach. Drug clientele right outside, alcoholics, prostitutes, killers, gamblers, robbers you name it, it was all outside any kind of street business you needed somewhere in the city had it. Every day was a different day. I was always thinking of ways to make money fast, as well as taking risks.

I was very fast at getting rid of my drugs, and re-upping became a habit. The money was fast, and sure. I kept on going like this until my age caught up with me. I got tired of all the fights with my boyfriend at the time, I got tired of taking my son with me everywhere I went, so I put him into daycare, and I enrolled into hair school.

At this time I'm still hustling crack cocaine, and weed at the same time. My supplier at this time is my partner, and friend who later becomes my husband. Not the boyfriend I was staying with, I hid them from each other for some years until that came out too. On days I was supposed to be in school, I was going to the spot where it all went down Decatur Street Northwest early in the morning I will drop my son off to daycare, and I will go over to the house and everything I was in need of was already there waiting for me to arrive.

My money, my man, my sex, my food, my business, and my nap time if I needed it. When I would get there, if I was hungry the home cook Jamaican food was already smelling good. Once I entered the house, the men had already had the food cooking from earlier that morning. This was done by the masterminds behind the scene of it all. Breakfast was good but lunch was like eating dinner, all at the same time people coming through buying what they needed. Picking up and dropping off went on until nighttime came.

The house shut down at a certain time, due to police watching and the place becoming hot. I missed a lot of school days being in this house. Once school hours have passed, I will go to the daycare to pick up my son. To only go back to my boyfriend's house where we were living, and it was my place to stay. Boyfriend had no clue I was gone all day with the man who became the love of my life at the time. Many days I will come back into the house, and my boyfriend would scratch his head, and pick fights, and arguments with me because he knew I didn't go to nobody's hair school.

Coming back with all this money, and drugs. Until one day my boyfriend put two, and two together. To understand there was a man Behind my come up. It went on until I got pregnant with my second child. The fights never stopped, as a matter of fact one day I got so tired of fighting him. I went to take my son for a walk on 13th Street NW. Darell follows me, and keeps asking me questions about my whereabouts, when I wasn't around him. I ignored him and kept walking with my son in my arms. He tried to snatch my son out of my arms from me, all I could do was pull my son's arms, and I began to bite the arm of Darell, until my tooth came out in his arm.

He let my son go, and me and my son kept it moving not to go back into his house until I cooled off. I was so mad I didn't even care about my tooth coming out. Me living with Darell at the time not having nowhere else to go I had to go back to his house.

Now me being pregnant with my second child hindered me from making my moves. At this time, I wasn't sure if the man I was living with was my baby's father or the man I was partnered with in my drug business was the father.

I had sex everyday with the both of them one would get me in the morning before leaving out or the night before. The drug partner would get me everytime we hooked up in the day, before I would go back to my Darell's house. I was trying to keep my business to myself. I wasn't sure what to do next at this time. I'm 20 years old, and I had to slow down on going to the drug spot everyday. My belly got bigger and bigger, so I automatically put the responsibilities of being my baby's father on Darell, I was staying with.

I couldn't go back to the streets, and my parent's house wasn't an option at all, to return to. By the time it was time for me to deliver the baby girl, I named her after Darell the man I was living with. My partner-in-crime wasn't nowhere to be found, plus he was playing it smooth with his children's mom. They were living in the same building as me and my Darell.

We lived in 503 and partner-in-crime lived with his children's mom in 303, in the same building. Now you know I couldn't bring no drama to this house, or else all

I was getting and depending on, from this Jamaican man was over, and dead. If this woman found out about little ole me with her baby daddy, it was going to be a lot of unnecessary foolishness. In which one day it was, she and my partner were coming in the elevator in which I and Darell were first.

She asked her baby father about me and him right there in the elevator. They begin arguing and fighting about me and him all the way down the hall and out the door they went. Throwing fist and each other. I learned how to wait on my man and let him run the show and play the game. Living a lie right in my face, and the face of others around us. I had to fake it to make it.

I was acting like I loved Darell, to keep my living arrangements secure at the time. Selling drugs to his mother to keep everybody happy as well as keep a place to stay over me, and my children's head. I was living my life as a gamble everyday. I remember getting into fights more, and more while pregnant, and living with Darell. I was living with him, and he still was very jealous, and insecure not wanting me to go anywhere without him. Every time I turned around, I was fighting him, or you would see hickeys all over my face, and neck, to make sure men would know I was taken.

One day at the Money house on Decatur street Northwest, I was in there chilling, and one of my boyfriend Darell's associates came in there to buy something, he sees me in there chilling laid back on the couch, feet up, and talking with the Jamaican guys. I saw him when he came in. I acted like I didn't even know him on this day when I went back to my Darell's house, and all hell broke loose between him and I.

By the time I got back into Darell's house acting innocent he had already gotten a call about me being with the Jamaicans on this day, so when I got back in, Darell began asking me a million, and one question. As to who, what, when, and where I was all day. Which caused me having to lie and deny where I truly was. I would say I went to school, that lie is what I stuck to. Well that's when the fight began all the way from the time, I got in the house till nighttime. I wouldn't admit that the man saw me earlier that day, in the Jamaicans house.

It seemed like every 20 minutes my Darell would ask me over, and over the same questions. Where was I coming from, who was I with, where did I get this money from, why you didn't go to school? I'm like look I don't know what you're talking about. I went to school, and the money I borrowed from a friend, of course he didn't believe that lie, none of what I said. As a matter of fact. He was sure I was with another man. His friend told him he saw me in the house. The fights would start up again because I wouldn't tell the truth.

Thank God for his mother, who would always come after 20 minutes of fighting and arguing to break up the fights. He would stay in his room, and I would go into the living room. This went on until one day I went to put my name on the waiting list for housing. Still living in their house I got tired of all the drama, and having to watch my back every time I left out the door.

Now I go into a shelter with my son, it wasn't as bad as I thought it would be. I had my own unit apartment, and I paid rent. This is where the road of having my own place began. I had my daughter at the age of 21 years old. At this time I'm living in southeast Washington DC in a building called 501 on the 5th floor. Another drug infested area. So from 1995 to 2002 I lived in this area until they moved us out, I had my second son in 1997 still living in southeast with my life going the way it was. Me selling drugs and different dudes in and out of my pants and life.

I had a hard time keeping up with the drama that I found myself in. So I raised my children in this area, and I lost a very good friend dear to my heart at this time of living down here. The Possession of evil in my life from my father's house was so intense, I can barely keep up with myself. One thing after the next kept happening to me, I survived it all thanks to God.

Keeping my mind through it all the runaway girl.

HOW I MADE IT...

CHAPTER TWO

They Said I was Hopeless

They said I was hopeless...

My own grandmother said to me in her living room of Floral street, Wheaton MD, one day. I would never live to be 18 years old. Thanks to God I did, and I'm living on in Jesus name.

They said I was hopeless...

Me not having the answer to why I was going through such a rough life I just didn't know or understand why me. Coming up in a dysfunctional home isn't always easy. Many challenges and obstacles are in front of your face, trying to get you to fear, and believe that what you see is normal, and what you're going through can't be told or talked about. So, you find yourself figuring out things by yourself, and the Holy Spirit. Who begins to crack the codes of everything in your past, bringing things back to your remembrance, and exposing the real enemies you're calling friends, and family.

They said I was hopeless...

Responsibilities, self-expectations, wanting approval of others, wanting to be the anchor for yourself and your siblings, as well as those around you, with the demonic attacks that comes your way. You can't explain why you start something and can't finish it. Why your life is Shifting, and you're not being able to change it at your own will. Witchcraft is real if you're not rooted and grounded in the Lord.

They said I was hopeless...

I'm so grateful to God for making me see the truth in my life, as well as having confirmation to almost all the things I went through. By a loved one confessing to me the unknown things done to me behind my back. Thanks to my cousin Rachel for letting me know I will get my life back after the death of my dad. Do to him playing with witchcraft and doing what he did to me in the presence of her mother at the age I was 10 years old. thanks God.

They said I was hopeless...

One of my days consisted of waking up in the morning, getting my sisters, and brothers, together for school, making sure hair was done, teeth brushed, fully dressed, and at the bus stop, or walking to school was on time. By then I had to help my mom get ready for work, finding her shoes, ironing her clothes, getting her medicine with a cup of water, so she can take it. Escorted her to her van watching her pull out and say yelling out the window to take something out for dinner. Me going back inside to take out chicken, to put in water. Then for me to get ready and go to school myself.

They said I was hopeless...

I got beat by my parents with belts, belt buckles, brooms, pots, pans, a gun put to my head, sitting in cold and hot water to get straight out, to being beat with the belt, and extension cord together. Writing a thousand times over and over again. Washing all the walls, standing on my head in the corner, cups being smashed on my head. Being beat naked until blood came out of my skin. Name calling, verbal abuse, these types of punishment made me change my mind real quick. To find a way out for myself.

They said I was hopeless...

I had to fix dad's dinner plate, wash his clothes, make his bed, and clean their room. Mom will come home from work and go straight to her video game, and there she stays, until the time for dad to come home. Then she will make sure I have done everything. While she made him think she did it all while he was at work.

They said I was hopeless...

Mom will play her Ms. Pacman game until she was ready to fall asleep, or she had to make a bathroom visit. That's when I made my mind up to run for it. I got tired of the same routine, and the abuse as well as not being appreciated. I would make my way to the basement to run away out the back door, or I will go out the window, whichever one wasn't boarded up with wood and nails.

They said I was hopeless...

Immediately running straight to DC. I would find a car to steal, ride it out till the gas runs out, going from neighborhoods to the drug strips. This was one of the ways I got around, on a daily basis. Possessed with witchcraft will have you doing things you never thought of doing. Real talk.

They said I was hopeless...

After getting caught by the police, for the crimes I was committing, as a juvenile. They would take me back to my parent's house, after 30 days I would run away again. It's like I couldn't stay in that house. Incest, abuse verbally, and physically, slavery, many fights and quarrels between me, and my siblings no happiness at all. Drinking bleach, trying to hang myself. God didn't let it work, the attacks from the demons would give me all kinds of demonic ideas to do to myself. They praying for an easy sacrifice as well as leave the tormentors looking innocent, and clean.

They said I was hopeless...

After all the years of watching my mom get beat and abused by my Dad. It's like she turned completely evil against me. Mom would always say you're a good fuck wasted. Dad would say you're not going to be shit in life. They would always tell my siblings not to be like me, she isn't going to be shit. They said I was hopeless. They made me feel like I wasn't meant to be born. Many times, I did ask God, why me? Why am I here? This is how I became friends with the streets.

 My own family didn't want me, only to use me for the work needed to be done around their house. Or to be a slave for their personal needs, like massaging mom's body till she fell asleep, being the babysitter, the housemaid along with many other things to fit their needs.

They said I was hopeless...

Now growing up with anger, witchcraft control, violence, and an alcoholic dad. I saw my dad beating my mom. I vowed I would never let a man beat me, and take advantage of me, and my children. I never wanted to be anything like my parents. I always said if I had children, I will treat my babies better than my mom, and dad treated me. I remember being made to drink 666 cough syrup, just because I got in trouble, not because I was sick. It was a form of punishment from dad, because it was so nasty. I remember my oldest sister trusting to tell me something so hurtful about my Dad that she couldn't trust nobody else to tell. Not even our mother. She said something told her to tell me. When I confronted him with my mom, I was put out of the house. They called the police on me, and said I was lying. My sister never got an apology nor was it addressed. It was put away like nothing never happened. So I apologized to her on behalf of our parents.

They said I was hopeless…

I remember coming back home from one of my runaway journeys, with this much older man I had met, and I had fun with him, and it was a good time away.

This time I came back with new clothes, new shoes, new bags, new underwear, the works. My man friend at the moment bought them for me at the time when he needed to make a run to New York. He asked me if I wanted to go. Of course, I said yes, and the highway we went 95 north. We only stayed for two days. Then I had to go back to my parent's house. The next day in my Dad's house every one of my right shoes was missing from each pair, he had brought me. I asked my sisters and brothers did they know what happened to them. Nobody seemed to know where my shoes had gone. This is another time he took something of my stuff to do witchcraft with it.

They said I was hopeless…

I remember Mom telling me when I was a baby, one day I wouldn't stop crying. So Dad took a safety pin, and stuck it in my leg, and said shut the hell up. He was drunk from alcohol, at the time of him doing this to me. Says my mom. Another excuse to cover up the abuse.

They said I was hopeless...

I think God for all the pain, abuse, abandonment, torment, tests, tears, and trials that I've been through. It made me a stronger person, and I've learned to not let people's words, evil works, or manipulations control who I am. God has the final say over my life. No matter what has been done to me, I've always kept GOD in my mind, and heart, death, hell, and the grave can't stop me. When I got into a car accident on my way to work from southeast DC to silver spring Maryland. I died in that moment and immediately I saw my Spirit on the clouds. I could see my three children in the house doing their usual routine. I instantly fell to my knees on this cloud pleading with God. Repenting, and telling God my children has no clue, I wouldn't be coming back home to them. Next thing I know my Spirit was shifted back into my body, and my head lifted off the steering wheel to a Caucasian man opening my jeep door. Asking me if I'm okay? This was nothing but GOD, that allowed me to come back to this natural life. That's when I realized God has a call on my life, that I have to answer to. Yahshua, and Jesus Christ alone is in control of my life. God has allowed many things to happen to me, that didn't kill me, or cripple my sanity. I can't explain why? I just know I'm chosen for a generation of people who will die to their flesh to do the work, and the will of ABBA Father the beginning and the End. Jehovah Jireh. GOD has been my provider through it all.

HOW I MADE IT...

CHAPTER THREE

THE STREET LIFE

I went from being in a foster family, to group homes, to the streets, to the jail, house to house, and being homeless on the streets. Sleeping in the snow, on the ground. Eating out of the trash can. At this point in my life, anything goes. I hit the streets at 15 years old, that was a very hard pill to swallow. With the torment, and the abuse from my parents. between the spirits running rapidly in the house, and nobody seeing them but me.

With the possessing Spirits making you do things; you know you didn't want to even think of doing. Waking up to your guilt of being in the mix of something that's not in your heart to do. Although you can explain how you got there, in the midst of confusion. Going back to my parent's house we are once called home. I found out this wasn't a home for me. I couldn't talk to no one, because I knew if I did, they would think I was crazy. For two reasons, one for exposing the people responsible to care for me.

Two no one else would tell the truth, to keep from the things happening to them.

So I kept it all to myself, and said that place is not an option for me, and my spirit to live and grow. Believe it or not I found my best peace, in the streets. There you knew what to expect. In the home things were happening all of a sudden unexpectedly. I just couldn't take it anymore. I got tired of all the Witchcraft games that were being played with my Spirit without my consent. I felt violated every time I found myself in something or doing something that wasn't in my will.

Once I left my father's house, all of my friends, and resources were gone. I looked around. I didn't have anybody to call on, or to get help I needed to understand my situation. Everything left me. No drugs to sell, no connections to link up with.

No food to eat, no money, nobody to talk to. I just would walk it down day by day. By riding the trains for free. Sleeping on the trains, and buses taking long rides, just because I had nothing else to do. This dry time in my life was very scary, and lonely, but God kept me every day and every night one day at a time.

By the printing office in Northeast Washington DC was my home for many days, and nights sleeping on Steam grate. My jacket was my pillow, and my sweater and clothes were my covers. I will call up into a bundle and wouldn't move until daybreak. I will go to this spot after I run the streets all night. It was a safe place for me, and nobody ever bothered me.

I thank God he would always take care of me and talk to me. To tell me where to go, and what to do even in my darkest moments of life. I remember waking up one morning, and my stomach was growling hungry for food. I had to go to the trash can, and pick through it. Thank God I found some good fresh food, picked over but edible. I tell you this was very uncomfortable for my spirit, and pride.

Sleeping on the cardboard boxes at times laying back, and thinking Lord what did I do to deserve this life? I heard the Lord tell me being prideful will do this to you. I thank God that I was able to break away from all that, and for him to deliver me, and give me my life back. In Jesus Christ name. I would have never in my dream, and thoughts would imagine me moving trash around in an outside trash can, looking for something to eat. Oh yes, I was humiliated, to the fullest.

This went on for like 2 weeks until one day, I woke up, and said I can stay like this. So, I went to the shelter. This shelter wasn't my cup of tea either. First of all, they gave me a curfew of 6 p.m. I didn't like that at all, it was too early for me to call it a night. The intake lady taking my information says to me, baby you look too young to be homeless. In my mind I'm thinking like okay, so what age is homeless appropriate? Anyway, I gave her my information, and she gave me the rules, and regulations of this shelter.

She then showed me around where my bed was, and where I will take my shower.

She handed me a heavy wool blanket. This place was very noisy, you can hear different conversations all at the same time. For some of the people there, this place looks like a drug rehab. The smell was very unkind, unwelcoming, stinky like Fritos feet, and dirty like butt that hasn't been washed for days. The smell was a bad mixture of spirits just plain out funky like they didn't wash for decades. So, with all that going on I decided, I'm not coming back to this place after this night.

The bathroom and the shower area were dirty. I had to get shower shoes yet and still I was so grateful for the water and the soap. I took my shower and went to my bed that night. I tried to make a phone call, and the line was so long like you are waiting in the jail to make a call, so I got tired of hearing all the arguments over who's next. I get out the line and decide to lay down. My sleep didn't meet me until 4 a.m. and all the people finally stopped talking and went to sleep. I woke up and breakfast time was 5 a.m. too early for anything at this time. Once I left, I didn't come back. I found myself back on the streets.

I remember waking up under the bed of a friend's house, the little brother would always catch me, and go running to tell his mom. Tanya's under the bed again. By the time his mom would make it to the room, I was already out the window, or out the back door. to face my day. I ended up going to another friend's house to get cleaned up, and maybe if I'm lucky get something to eat.

Once I finish, I will leave there, and start my day depending on the weather, which is how I will make my next move. On a rainy day I would chill inside of Union Station walking the mall.

On a hot day anything goes, but at this point I wasn't smoking weed yet. I was only drinking beer after getting the drinks in me. A good day was like this, I will be on the drug strip, depending on what Hood I was in. That day I will re-up on my drugs, and go sell them off between 6 p.m. or 9 p.m. All my drugs must be sold off. I never went back in the house wherever I was staying with my drugs. In the night only money goes back with me. As the night falls it's time to start figuring out where I will lay my head for the night depending on what area of the town, I was in.

I will start to look for someplace to sleep, oh well if I didn't find any place to go I will ride the trains all night till I get my sleep off. Then wake up, and back to the same routine just a different day. I remember when I was 12 years old, I was in New York City Brooklyn. I was in this apartment building with big drug dealers, and prostitutes. This is where I learned how to cook crack. I see the hardcore street life really for what it was. The parties were like no other parties, I had ever gone to.

They will start at 10 p.m. and don't finish till 7 a.m. The sun comes up, and the music is still jamming on, and people still partying like nobody's business. This was definitely like no other place I have been before money was being made all night long. I thought the people there never slept. I had to be very careful as to what group I will find myself in. It's nothing like DC where I was able to go anywhere.

In New York you better stick to the gang, or groups of people that accept you. Once you're in there isn't No outs unless you move out the state. Like I did I'm so grateful to God for the experience I had from the street life at a young age, because once I started having my own children I definitely knew not to grow them up in New York the fast lane is a bit too much at times. I thank God for protecting me from state to state in my travels with strangers.

One day on this brisk snowy cold night. It came down hard on me unexpectedly this time. I didn't know I wasn't going to have anywhere or shelter to sleep in DC. Well it seemed like time wasn't on my side. The day was gone so fast before I knew it night had come upon me. I wasn't thinking fast enough to figure out who was going to hold me down for this night.

After walking the streets, and going about trying to find a man to pick me up, and take me in. No luck. No one stopped to pick me up. No nothing this particular night. I had to find a spot on the ground. Only my jacket and clothes I had on my back to keep me warm. The snow began to come down harder, and fast the streets were dark like a GHOST town. It looked like everybody left the streets but me. I was in NE. I found this grate with the hot air blowing up it. I laid a cardboard box flat over top of it. Next was my body going on top of it. It me a few minutes to fall asleep.

Eventually I drifted off ignoring the snow, cold, and all. I remember days I needed a car to get around, and I didn't have any money to buy my own. I will catch a ride all the way to Wheaton Maryland early in the morning like around 6 a.m. I will walk the streets until I pick which car, I was going to take that day. The people would have their cars warming up, and keys still in the ignition. I will go, get in their car, and start my errands. Getting things done, I couldn't do it on foot. This car became mine for at least a week.

If I didn't get caught by the police first. This is truly a sign of Witchcraft, doing something you know is wrong, but your mind is not functioning under the will of God. Being possessed by demons is what this is called. I remember taking my last $125 to sacrifice it to get a 8-ball. Cut it up, and before you know it, I was in the hood selling them Stone till at least all were gone.

When the sale flow got slow. I will go to another neighborhood and post up or give a drug addict some for free, just to get it all sold off fast. Some days are better than others. I found out just because I was selling the drugs. I wasn't any better than the one using it. The stronghold of the enemy had me too. I had an addiction to selling it. I was just like them, possessed with a demon.

I didn't know it at the time. I felt like I was normal just trying to find ways to survive. It all started from worldly temptations and needing money for my day to day needs and necessities. Flesh and worldly desire, and suddenly I began to do this on a regular basis selling drugs became a habit and I was overtaken by The Works of Satan demonized without me noticing. However, the devil was working his way through my life during this time, and I didn't even know it by the influences of the patterns and the decisions I was making out of the will of God. I think God daily, for my Deliverance I thank God for teaching me how to maintain my Deliverance.

I remember going to the Trap House once I got in there it was all full of Guys. They weren't happy to see me because they knew my product I was selling was better than theirs, and I will get all the sales, once I got one of the addicts to smoke what I had they would instantly begin working for me.

That's how good my product was. I would never get my stuff from the same people the Guys in the hood would buy their products from.

I always had an outside link that was not connected in the neighborhood. Inside of this trap house is crap games going on in different groups. People getting high in the bathroom. People drinking and smoking and doing them in their own zone. I came in to try to sell my drugs. Hours passed and the place started to clear out. Only ones left in this place at nighttime are the neighborhood drug boys and me. The addicts have gone about their business.

I thought I was okay, in there with them smoking weed, and drinking Remy Martin. It's like they put everyone out except for me. Then with me always hanging with the fella's I didn't think anything would happen to me. Next thing I knew I was being dragged in the bedroom. When they got me inside, I looked around, and there were six dudes all circling around the bed one of them grabbed me and threw me down on the bed. I jumped up, and he slapped the mess out of me with his pistol. He said to me you know what it is.

Shut up before we duct tape your mouth and tie you up. Next thing I knew he began pulling down my pants, like he was ripping them off me while I'm on the bed. I'm kicking, and screaming he's holding my mouth, and said I will hit you again with the pistol in your face. I felt the fear of them killing me. So, at this point I didn't try to move and make any more noise. I remember crying while they are taking turns rapping me, I asked them why are you doing this to me? They told me to shut the fuck up before it got worse.

Each one of them took turns having sex with me until they all climaxed. As they finished, they would leave out the room one by one. I had no choice but to let them do what they wanted to do to me or else I would be left in this back room in Sursum Corda's dead. I'm sure you can imagine everything else. I was left in the room crying, and in so much pain. Once the last one left out, I got up, and went to the bathroom to clean myself up.

I had marks on my face and bruises on my body. The side of my face was swollen from the gun, hitting my face. I looked like I got jumped, and the hell beat out of me. When I came out of the bathroom not a soul was in this trap house. Everybody was gone. I left this place and couldn't tell anybody. I felt like if I went to the police I would get killed. So, I decided to leave this hood and didn't return to it for years. Police wasn't an option for me. I believed in the street codes.

I remember each one of them for a long time, and I never saw any of them after this incident occurred. I do believe GOD punished each one of them very quickly. That's just my thought. This was one of the saddest days of my life being on the streets. From this I lost a lot of boldness especially when it comes to being around dudes by myself.

I Remember being on Kennedy Street Northwest, and I was minding my business selling my drugs out of nowhere these girls came on the block to jump me and started fighting me trying to take my money and drugs from me.

I fought them off until someone came and broke them up off me, they were after my money, and drugs. They couldn't get to it. I had it stashed in my pants. So, they left before the police came.

I got myself together. I was okay when the police came, and I didn't talk to them. I acted like I wasn't the one who was fighting. I was throwing the police off when they started asking me questions. Nobody said nothing, and eventually they left the block. My supplier came to pick me up and put me into a hotel for the night so I could be safe. Boy was I glad to be in the hotel safe by myself, and I didn't have to have sex to sleep that night he left me there by myself.

I remember not having no drugs to sell the dude I was getting my drugs from got locked up. I had nothing else to do but start selling my body. I cleaned myself up, and I began to take car after car, man after man. I worked all night until I made enough to put me in a hotel for two days. Just enough to buy me some re-up drugs from somewhere, some food to eat, and an outfit to wear. I never enjoyed selling my body or having the sex with these different men. It never was pleasure; it was always business. In my mind it was my easy way to get money back into my hand surviving day-by-day when I need to.

Well riding around in stolen SUV's was part of the reason I spent most of my time in jail amongst some other things. Many people would take my looks and try to take advantage of me. The streets made me strong, and fear left me a long time ago. Due to all the things I had encountered in the streets to survive. This definitely isn't all the things I have encountered in the experiences of living and surviving the streets.

It's just enough to let you know as the reader that life wasn't no joke for me growing up. I had no idea this street life would be so hard for me to survive and stay alive. The struggle in the streets is real. Only the strong survive. Today I've been delivered set free from witchcraft, demonic influences, possession, and Temptation. My body has been healed after forgiving everybody through the blood of Jesus Christ.

My mind is now under the influence of Jesus Christ, and Yahushua Hamashiach I'm reading my Bible daily. I'm helping as many people as I can. By giving what I have and my real-life testimonies, and experiences that I've survived by God allowing me to Live Another day. I thank God for renewing my mind, and changing my heart to the fear in the heart of God I'm free from everyone who played a part in hurting me, abusing me, using me, lying on me, rejecting me, and trying to take my life from me. God allowed me to forgive all the people in my life.

What I've learned through it all is God was with me in the good, and the bad times in my life. Whatever the devil meant for evil God made for my good. I've released everyone who has ever hurt me, in any kind of way. I had to forgive everyone. So that God could forgive me of all my sins known and unknown. The hurt, betrayal, and the pain are there. I choose not to care. I leave all that concerns me to the faithful God who's always been there.

Being that person in a car accident ended up on those clouds. Changed my whole perspective of life. I'm not my own but I'm the one on borrowed time till the creator sends for me. Please don't take your life for granted.

Your living because GOD has placed purpose in you. Humble yourself, and ask GOD what is it he would like for you to do? My wicked ways had to depart from me, and I had to detach myself from my family's lineage of sin. So I could be used by God for him to get all the glory.

Since dying and coming back to this life I've been so scared to leave the will of GOD. Nothing else matters now. I'm not influenced by nothing this wicked world has to offer. I'm sold out for my Alpha and Omega the Beginning and the End. ABBA Father is his name. My first assignment is to pray and guide my children in the fear of GOD. Teaching them to follow the 10 commandments that were left with basic instructions before leaving this earth.

I've had to gain self-control and Deliverance from GOD to change my heart and put a new song in my mouth despite all the wrong I've done, and all the wrong that was done unto me. I'm a living walking testimony of the Grace and Mercies of God made new every morning.

GOD has put his words in my mouth and made me his wonderful tangible transformation.

I'm so grateful for the Lord choosing to use me for my generation and abroad to show and to prove he's a keeper from all generational curses, iniquities, hatred jealousy, anger, unforgiveness murder, sexual immorality, Alcoholism, drug addiction, witchcraft, sorcery, magic adultery divination, division, heresy, initiation into sex, oaths Covenants, pack, rejection, abuse, sacrifices made, manipulated by Satan and his agents from the kingdom of darkness. I'm forever covered by the powerful Blood of Jesus Christ and Yahshua Hamashiach Amen..

HOW I MADE IT...

Chapter Four

SINGLE MOTHER

SPERM DONOR, FATHER, CHILDREN

Two Boys & Two Girls...

Being a single mother isn't something I planned on being. Running the streets and ending up in different types of situations, led up to me being the best single parent I could be for my children, who didn't ask to come to this world. None of my pregnancies were planned, they just happened. My first pregnancy I thought I had the right sperm donor. Once the test was done it came out it was not who I thought it was. After the embarrassment of getting the wrong man. I gave up on looking.

My second pregnancy had me caught between two men. I let them both know I was pregnant, and neither denied the baby but I had to make a decision based on my living arrangements. As well as what was best for me, at the time of raising my children. Let me tell you, I made a big mistake out of this whole issue. By naming the child. On top of living in the man's house just for a place to stay.

Once I was able to move out and get my own place, I was able to let the truth out. It made me look like a fool. Living my life, the best I could with what I had at hands reach.

This is how I was living once upon a time. Doing whatever needed to get done to get by. So, don't fault me is the way I was looking at it. I told the truth of me having sex with both partners. On the same day one in the morning and one in the night. It wasn't me; they were monitoring my goodies.

All day every day for a season of my life this went on. Anyway, once I got married to my husband, he accepted all my children as his own children.

This was already in the making before my marriage, because we spent so many years together. My husband had me in his hands since I was 15 years old. I remember taking my oldest son to him when he was 8 months old. At the time my husband wasn't my husband he was my partner like Bonnie, and Clyde I was his right-hand girl. He said to me you have a handsome boy here Tanya not knowing at the time this man will be the one helping me raise all my children.

The time of him being in my life for so long, when I first met this man, he was 27 years old. By the time I introduced him to my oldest I was 18 years old. I disappeared from the streets for a while to have my baby and get situated at my parent's house for just a little while. Not knowing what I was signed up for all in one nutshell. This man right here was very sweet, and what he did to me in bed I used to call him sweet. I'd rather not say the rest.

I must say for the time he was active in my life he has been a friend, a lover, a father, a brother, sperm donor, friend, enemy all in one. This has been a Bittersweet moment in my life. I thought me and him were going to be till death do us apart. I really did love him more than any man I had ever met so in my mind at the time, me and this man will never come to an end. Therefore, I thank God for being in control of my life because I didn't know what was good for me at the time. I thought all the money, cars, clothes, trips along with the monthly maintenance he kept up for me was life living life the best way, so I thought I was brainwashed by his actions, and deeds to me.

I got so used to him taking care of me I couldn't see myself with another man. Especially when he tells me if a man can't take care of you like I do don't waste your time with him.

I thought I was set for the good life little did I know. As I matured and grew up I had begun to realize this was a ride to hell and back to heaven after it's all said and done from being in hell to give him my life back to God so that I can live out longer than all my friend enemies, like this main one who stayed so close yet so far. This in the beginning was a Bonnie, and Clyde thing. Street Partners, to parents, and in my mind always lovers.

Love unconditionally is what I had for this man. That love will always overpower the bad. I found out that time heals all wounds. As I write this chapter it's all bittersweet. Well from the time I put my son in his arms. I told him that I couldn't take him back to my parent's house, at the time of that night. He put us in a hotel that night. In my mind I knew I had to find a safe place for me, and my baby. Time went on until I settled in my own place. In southeast 501 apartment 503 now I got my third child. This is definitely a cappers man who helped me make this Third child my second son.

The ones who I had tested weren't the father. I have one more who I believed to be his dad, but he stayed in jail, so the test is out of the question to me. I don't feel comfortable pointing my finger at any other man to find a dad for my son. I'll tell him I apologize for my foolishness but at this time God is your father so this child I raised him by myself as the rest, but he did get what little love from my ex-husband when he was around. I must say my ex-husband did really love all my children in my eyes, he would do for me, and them.

So, I have no clue who is the father of my third child. I tell you I know God as my father, my provider, my comforter, my peace, my guidance, my Everything. So, I teach my son that God is his father. If he wants him to know his sperm donor, God will reveal it to him. The Holy Spirit reveals everything, all you must do is ask. Now after 19 years I waited to have another baby.

Thank God by this time my life is more settled. I'm not risking myself going from man to man. This one is an African man he didn't ask for me, and I sure didn't ask for him. I happen to be on a dating app. Out of the line of men I had to pick from my spirit told me to pick this man. I did, after some months dating him, having sex I got pregnant with his baby. I had no clue I would have another child at this time, me being 41 years old in my life. I was working and maintaining my three children already.

They were all living at home with me during this time. Thank God they were my help I had by my side. The children were happy, and excited about a new baby, so they didn't mind having another sibling. The father on the other hand, he did mine. He did not want the baby. He gave me $450 to go and have an abortion. He dropped me off in front of the abortion clinic early in the morning, with my daughter. He left me there to get the procedure.

Well when the office opened at 9 a.m. I went to open the door, and they had a lady come to the door. She told me I can't get any service from them. I called around trying to get this done this day. It didn't work, I also heard the Lord tell me not to push the fire of killing this baby. I let it go and said okay I will have it. I called the father the same day to tell him, I couldn't get it. He let me know, he lost his job the same day. He was working for the government during this time.

I decided to keep my baby. I started back to work the next day and began to look for prenatal care. Soon after some months, my friends, and family put together a baby shower for us. This was a spiritual pregnancy, from the very beginning to me. One I never worked bearing any of my children. This one I worked everyday, until the time for her to come out. The doctor predicted that she would be delivered by February 14th. God's due date was January 2015. I thank God for reversing any curses that were sent to me, and my baby. Once it's time for me to deliver her, I couldn't do a normal delivery.

The umbilical cord was wrapped around her neck, and her body at the same time labor had to induce. The Lord told me nobody, but my children could be with me at the time of my delivery and I wasn't to tell nobody not even the father. The father was calling and blowing up my phone on this day. I didn't answer him until 10 days after the baby was delivered. I stayed in the hospital with her by myself day, and night on the 10th day we went home, and her father was able to lay eyes on her for the first time.

I've learned the hard way through past experiences, how to listen to my spirit especially when I hear the Lord talking first and clear.

At this point in my life I've been through hell, and back so I'm not easy to be fooled. I know what I know when I'm seeking the Lord before making any decisions and moves. God instructed me step-by-step what to do and say when things concerning this child.

Thank God I wasn't smoking, and drinking during this time so to see clearly, and my situation was good for me.

I had a tough time giving birth, but once I started praying for us all things began to flow the way it was ordained. God is faithful Even in our mess, what the devil meant for bad God changed it for my good. I remember giving her father all my old shoes, purses, clothes, and all my babies old clothes and things. To send to his country to the orphans there. What he did with them, I don't know. He claims he sent them to Cameroon to help the poor less fortunate young girls. I pray that's where they ended up but oh well, if it didn't my intentions were right.

I didn't need them anymore, and they were all in good condition still. I felt I was being a blessing to some others only God knows what he did when he took those things from my home. This baby is different from the way when I was asked by her dad to pierce her ears. I went to try to pierce her ears, and the Holy Spirit came to me, and said don't Pierce her ears. I felt the spirit so strongly, I could only listen.

The second time I was in the mall walking past Claire's accessory store, I went in, and again the Spirit came to me, and said I said don't Pierce her ears. I was like Wow looking at my daughter like you're very special to God. Whatever assignment God has for her I can't do anything but nourish it in the fear of God.

As I got older, I got better as a parent as a mom, as a sibling. In my eyes me, and my children are siblings in the eyes of God so raising them is different especially when they have different DNA other than mine.

However, with the oldest now, I try to work with them as siblings, so we don't perish like fools. God is our parents, our mom, and dad. I seek the Lord concerning them, so we have this new member, and we all have a role in her life. If they choose to be. All my children are blessings to me. I'm grateful for all The Good the Bad, and the Ugly. I've learned to appreciate them by the way I was treated by my parents, family and friends. All this mistreatment to me made me want to be the best mom I could be for them. They didn't ask to come into this world. It's all a product of my sin I must take full responsibility and try my best to show them to live a God-fearing life.

As I realize I'm not perfect, and I'm a different person than who I once was. Weather under possession of negative influences. I've had to let go and let God. Being a single mom isn't easy. I made many mistakes with my oldest children. I've shown them things I should have kept to myself. I have hurt them in ways I should have loved them and did things differently. I'm older now, all I can do is repent for my stupidity. The hurt, and pain that I have caused in their life verbally, and physically. I pray they forgive me.

This fourth child has been tampered with since the age of five months. Her sperm donor put something in the back of her neck. I was washing dishes one day when he came to visit her, I gave her to him to hold. He went into the living room, and was facing the window, at a distance from where I was in the kitchen. Out of nowhere, I hear my baby burst out crying, in my spirit is saying he did something to her.

I ran over to him, and yelled at him, and said what the hell have you done to my baby? He replied Tonya here take your baby. I don't know why she's crying. He was lying, as I began to pray, and fast asking God what this man do to my baby. A year goes by and the Holy Spirit tells me to look at the back of her neck, then when I look, the spirit says to me he put something in there. Yes, indeed when I look at the back of her neck, there is a mark, a bump like protrude Circle. This is a mark from his culture, from Cameroon.

I was told by his own kind of people, that this is how they identify with their children when they get older it can help him monitor her in the spirit.

I plead the blood of Jesus Christ over her life she will forever be controlled by the Lord Jesus Christ. The Holy Spirit in Jesus name amen as a result of this I noticed how she does things she knows is wrong to provoke me to anger. Thank God I'm changed. I don't react to the things she does. I fix it and pray I also make her know what is going on whether she is wrong or right.

Some things I noticed are not done intentionally, but she does it, so I make her be accountable for her actions. When she is older, she will not be doing things saying she's not aware of her actions. I pray over my children; I commit them to the blood of Jesus Christ. I pray for our Unity, and for God to forgive us of all our sins. That God's Will be done in our lives. I read the bible with them and teach them to fear the Lord. I try my best to let them be who they are, and trust God they will find their way in the righteousness of God.

Keeping his Commandments, and showing the world whatever, we go through, good or bad to give God all the glory, honor, and praise. A lot of things happen to show us ourselves to make us feel convicted and change from our wicked ways. Only what we do for Christ will last. I remembered thinking I was always right, to find out I was wrong. I had to ask for forgiveness because God's ways are not like our ways nor his thoughts like our thoughts. God will check mate me and tell me to apologize.

The Holy Spirit is the only true teacher. He will correct and chastise you if you're out of order. I thank God for being my mom, and dad when I was parentless. God is faithful above all matters.

HOW I MADE IT...

Chapter 5

TIME TO CHANGE...

DEATH OF CLOSE LOVE ONES AND FRIENDS.

    I remember going to a girlfriend's house party, in Greenway Southeast. I took my three children with me to this party. I knew they would be in the back room with all the other children, while we the parents were partying in the front room. It was a great game changer in my life at the time. I've got to meet my new man to be at the time.

The late Ronald Scriber Jr. This man walked into this apartment with a few of his other male friends with him. Immediately me and him looked at each other, and instantly I knew he was going to be mine. I just felt it in my Spirit. I quickly went to my girlfriend to tell her before the party got started that the light skinned guy in the front was mine.

I put claims on him immediately. Ronnie is what they called him. Thick, nicely groomed fresh in dress, and hair cut is sharp. Looking good from head to toe. He was the leader in his group, and in his character. That made me even more attractive to him. I knew this was my kind of man.

Once I got the children situated in the back room with the other children, it's now my time to get acquainted with this handsome man. This man caught my eyes the moment he stepped into the room.

Oh yeah just like I thought. He came straight to me once I came out the back room and started asking me questions about myself.

Now this was one good house party, he had the weed, the Remy Martin drinks, and the money honey... He also had the drugs for his clients that were blowing up his phone, while we were getting acquainted. He immediately began to let me know he didn't have a girl. That I didn't have to worry about any other woman. He wanted me to be his woman. This was moreover easier than I expected.

He told me anything I needed and wanted him to make it happen for me. First things first, I let him know I was going to need a ride home with my children after this party is over. He said to me you got it. Is that all you need? I said yeah for now. I didn't want to be too needy, just meeting him at my girlfriend's house party.

The music was loud, people were partying, drinking, dancing, socializing, and having a good time. While the whole night Ronnie and I stayed by each other the whole-time chilling, talking and enjoying each other's company. Meeting him I felt so comfortable, as if I knew him before tonight. Our Spirit just connected with no problem.

He was a Leo, and so was I. His birthday was around the last of July. Mines was in August in the middle. Everything went so smooth with us. It was unbelievable to me, but I was going with the flow of the vibes. Before you know it Ronnie was asking me, are you ready to get the children in the house? I was shocked it wasn't even late.

He didn't want me, and my children there any longer. So, I said yes I'm ready when you are. He called my girlfriend over to us and told her I was going with him. I felt so secure with him. She was smiling from ear-to-ear, although I got The Vibes, she wanted him too. Oh well it's too late for that, he's mine now is what I was thinking in my head.

I went to the room and called my children to leave the party. I said my goodbyes to everyone, and myself the children and Ronnie headed straight for the door. Ronnie had his own car so before he left with me and my children, he let his friends know he was taking me home. I heard him tell them he would be right back in a few.

He took me and my children right to our door 311 L Street Southeast. He then kissed me on my cheek and said don't go to sleep I'm going to call you once I get to my Mother's house. I stayed up all night bubbling. I was so happy it was something different about this young man, but I couldn't put my hand on it right away. I just knew I was going to be good with him by my side, a real Survivor.

He was the type of guy that was so nice but if you tried to get it twisted. He was going to twist you. He was a Leo like me July 28th me August 17th two Leo's boy did we have our time. Once he introduced me to his parents and sister and brother. I didn't think they liked me all because I already had three children in what they called an already made family.

Oh well he loved me, and I loved him, we were Unbreakable he told me my children were his children. I got pregnant with his child. He begged me to abort and I couldn't understand it. I was working at the DMV on C Street Northwest at the time he told me if I would have the baby, he was going to be mad and he would break up with me.

I couldn't understand this, he said my children were like his children, he loves them like he loves me and that I didn't need any more kids at the time. I thought about this real hard and I said okay let me do what he wants so I made the appointment at the abortion clinic and he took me the very next day to have this procedure done.

Once I did the abortion this man was treating me nicer than he's ever treated me before I got pregnant. He took me shopping and at this point he wanted me to get his name tatted on me.

I was scared I never had a tattoo before, but I was so in love I didn't think twice. I said okay to it. He then takes me to the off the hook tattoo place off Pennsylvania Avenue Southeast. He paid for it. This was very painful.

I didn't want anything too big, so I just got his name in a heart on my left arm. Ronnie was smiling from ear-to-ear, He said you're going to be my wife. I was sliced the love, and the compassion we had, for each other was like something I never experienced in my life at the time. Ronnie was a do him type of guy. He was a leader. He never followed anyone. He made his own choices for himself.

As we were dating time went on until I asked him to move in with me, and he did. Of course, his mom didn't want that for him, but he came. I was the one cooking his food washing his clothes and making sure he was good. In every area a woman is supposed to take care of her man. It was more secure with him in the same house as me.

Plus, I felt better not being jealous if he stayed out late. I knew he was sleeping next to me every time. I can't lie, I feel so deep in love with this man. I began stocking him once he'd be out all night. I was hooked on him. So, him moving in was his way of proving to me it wasn't any other female besides me that he loved, and to prove it wasn't nobody else in his gaze.

He didn't have a job at the time the streets were how he made his money. He got deeper and deeper in the street life drug selling and then he began to smoke the Dipper PCP in my eyes he will control himself good under the influence I tried to get them to stop and also got him to accept Jesus Christ as his savior.

I remember one day in our room the Holy Spirit hit me and said read the Bible with him and take him through the Sinners prayer he did. He repented for his sins, and accepted Jesus as his savior Romans 10 and 9. It seems like not soon we did that our relationship started getting on fire more, and more fights, we were having. It seemed like things were getting worse.

Our fights are over petty stuff, every time he would try to leave me, he would come back home. The love we had for each other was true. Maybe a little violent, but I loved him, and he loved me no matter what people said to him about me. I remember one day we were fighting in our room and the gun went off. My goodness I was scared, white powder went everywhere I hurried up, and told the children not to say anything to anybody once the police came out.

Thank God for his man. He got to us before the police did and got rid of the gun. Ronnie took the beef, but when I saw they were trying to keep him for a long time. I had to tell them he didn't do anything and eventually he was released. I thought this was the end of us but no, he came home to me. I believe we had a Fatal Attraction for each other. I wouldn't dare get caught talking to another man about nothing.

Ronnie was all I needed in a man he did the best he could do with me, and my three children. The night of his death I felt it in my belly. I knew something was wrong with him. I just couldn't put my hand on it. My little sister was living with me at the time I got dressed in all black and I told her to watch the children don't let nobody in the house, I will be back. I got in my truck and started driving all around.

I knew he would be looking for him all night. No sign of Ronnie out of nowhere I got a call from his mom telling me Ronnie was killed. I started screaming to the top of my lungs and hitting my head on the steering wheel. I wouldn't stop screaming and hitting my forehead on the steering wheel. Saying No No No not my Ronnie. Well low and behold I ended up in front of the house of my old school mate.

He came to my truck to see if I was ok and before I knew it, he was consoling me and telling me to come into his house. I went but once I got myself together, I had to leave and go back home to tell my sister.

I wasn't hallucinating about what I was feeling in my belly about Ronnie. This all happened right after my birthday. He died August 21, 2000. I went into a deep depression after his death. His family didn't acknowledge me in the obituary. They put some other girl. It was cool we all knew the real deal when he was living. However, I paid it no attention at all. His mom set off doves at his funeral.

The same doves came by over my house the same night. I remember hearing the Spirit tell me to get up and go outside to the front door and look up. I looked up and it was the white doves flying over my house. I ran to the back door to see them off, I was crying because I knew that was Ronnie saying his last goodbyes to me. On that day I realized why he didn't want me to have his baby.

The baby is now with him on the other side. It's like he didn't want to leave nothing of himself behind. What a tough pill to swallow I also found out witchcraft was behind this too. In which it didn't surprise me. God revealed everything to me people thought I was crazy, but the Lord confirmed what he showed me 5 years later due to the voice of my cousin pleading not guilty on her, and her mom's part, but putting it all on my dad.

I said all y'all hands are dirty every one of y'all. I'm going to leave it right there. I do believe if he was alive today, he would be my husband, the love we shared was unbreakable. People couldn't understand it for the life of them, he didn't care, and neither did I of course. He made me happy, and I kept a smile on his face. Plus, he was sucker free. A provider, and a protector, a real man. Oh, Ronnie you are forever missed.

Always in my mind and dreams. Until one day I came out of the three-year deep depression behind his death. His spirit came for me. I had to tell him to stop visiting me. I had myself, and my three children to live for. I told him I will see you when my job here on earth is done for God, and my family. I refused to entertain his death Spirit. It was the witches using his face during the visitations in my dreams.

Whenever they came, they wanted me to come on that side of death. Nope God got me. I will not die an untimely death. When the good Lord is finished with me then I believe we will meet again not before in Jesus Christ name amen. However, I had to discontinue the mourning of his death, and the visitations from whoever they were.

Now in my life at this time God will use me to have a word of encouragement for the young guy around me and in my neighborhood I would have awkward time with them and the Holy Spirit when I'm getting them to repent and seek God Lil Charles Dub C was also one of the dear young guys to my heart I used to do his hair for him I started his dreadlocks and he will come to get me every so often to get his discount price for his locked to be done he was a good young man just moving and growing fast in the drug world oh well God Rest his soul.

Bubbles was another one I had the opportunity to always talk to about God, and his saving Grace. It all would happen in awkward moments, only if the streets weren't so mean, and heartless I do believe they will still be here. Although I had to come to terms, God don't make any mistakes he had need of them. To be absent from the body is to be present with the Lord. However, I can't question any of it.

I just let it leave a loving memory, and keep it moving. I'm glad I was God's messenger. All the lost souls he had me speak to, I used myself as an example that God can change anybody if you really wanted to be changed. I would like a mom, a sister, an aunt they never had. I'm grateful to the souls alive and Sleep God used me for, may he get his glory.

Wow Big George was another one the sex was the bomb he had that New York's swag mixed with a little DC, isn't going for nothing. The drugs took him he had some of the best weed on the market at one time he was well-known and respected he was set in his own way sex drugs and money you couldn't change that so I just would enjoy him all I could every chance we got.

I remember getting pregnant by him, so he paid for the abortion because his baby mother down the street just had a baby by him and he didn't want any problems, so we got rid of it. Not to mention I thought my youngest son was his, but the test said no I watched him try to get himself together then he will be back at his same old tricks but this time deeper and on harder drugs. We had our last talk.

I knew he was gone; he went out hard by getting high on hard drugs. He had a good heart, if he liked you; you were good on getting whatever you wanted from him. May God rest his soul.

I remember Jeremiah, this young pretty girl who was locked up with me at the receiving home she was doing her getting money prostituting along with a few other gigs. When God took her, I was scared straight to see a young girl go just like that I began to seek the Lord and change my life for the good. Me seeing and being around all this death I had to make a choice of life or death for myself.

I knew I had my children so the love for them made me get myself together and stop selling drugs to stop tricking for money and just go cold turkey for God. it wasn't easy at all even when I thought I had it all together before you knew it, I was backsliding. God please forgive me for all my sins going to church and coming home smoking weed.

I was still having sex I haven't been completely delivered from my own demons yet. Getting up and falling straight on my face became a habit to me. I learned how to survive. I was too scared of God to do too much; I was just doing enough to get to the next level. Whatever it was for whatever I needed I knew how to get it in and get out.

Thank God for not taking me in my sin. God has been so faithful he's protected me from many dangers, and he sheltered me when I had no places to lay my head or my children's head. God has fed me when I had no food. God has been my peace of mind when the devil tried to make me lose my mind.

I remember hitting the PCP for the second time this was the last time for me. I was in Cappers as a matter of fact it was before Ronnie died, I hit one with him. Once I hit that cigarette, I started hallucinating, I thought the money I got from selling my drugs was fake. I started ripping all my money up in the middle of the street.

They got me in the house and poured milk down my throat. When I finally came back down from this high. I said never again bad boy drug is too much for me. That was the last and final time for me, and the dippers as they called them back then. I truly thank God for sending my angel in human form into my life. I remember my children got taken from me buy (CPS) Child Protective Services.

The Lord let the counselor see who I was in the spirit, and she helped me get my children back for good as well as she stayed my friend after the case was closed. She would say this is not the time nor the place just believe keep God's face I had to learn how to wait on the Lord. Every time I tried to do it my way something would set me back.

Besides I had to learn the hard way I had no real friends, they only wanted friendship if it benefited them, besides they are being jealous of me. I always made it look easy. Getting money and staying fly was a habit. I made the outside look good while the whole time I was as black as Black inside not knowing I was going deeper, and deeper into hell. One day I had an outer body experience about hell.

Hell is real, I remember I was around all the fire I saw heads detaching from their bodies and parts of the bodies being snatched apart by itself. A lot of screaming and crying real loud all in the mist in the lake of fire.

I was by this tree kneeling, crying scared when my turn was coming, and I remember crying to God. I was dirty in rags, and two angels in white came by me with a stretcher and said get on, the father has need of you.

This was another moment I got scared straight by God. I didn't want to end up back in hell, so I went back to God again trying my best to get it right. No matter how much I tried to stay out of trouble it seemed to find me a way. Willingly or unwillingly through it all God has been my keeper. Thank you, Jesus Christ who is the head of my life I've always had a heart, for God.

I didn't intentionally just wake up and do bad. I will find myself into stuff I didn't even ask for. Although I wasn't a snitch or a sucker, I handle whatever came my way, to the best of my ability. With God before me who can be against me. No matter what you find yourself in if it's not of God you must repent immediately.

Get yourself back on the right path of thinking and moving. When you know better you do better.

God is faithful, you must be true to thine own self, Pray for God to put the purpose of his will for your life in your heart and mind. Only what you do for Christ will last. Don't waste your time on people. Be your own motivation, push yourself to higher heights. Don't stay in the same place too long. Read the word of God and search your heart to do what's inside of you to be a help to someone else. Be a blessing in yourself lesson.

Losing my mom was a hard pill to swallow. I loved her so much, but we didn't have a good relationship. I'm her seventh child. I'm grateful for being her daughter. I learned a lot from my mother, good and bad. I appreciate God for using me to be her spokesperson, I had no problem speaking up and backing her up whenever she needed me to. Things she feared I approached head on for her in the Spirit, and in the natural.

I tried my best to understand my mom once I had children of my own. Some things I took with me in my memory and some things about her I deleted. Things I knew I would do differently as a mom and a woman. She was a very strong woman in many areas of her life. She had so many jealous of her, by the way she looked, dressed, and was educationally blessed.

My mom had it going on until the love of her life took her for granted, and she began to fall weak to the devil. The way she allowed that man to use and abuse her. I wouldn't never in my lifetime let a man treat me that way. It was unbelievable the abuse and misery she dealt with along with the fear she allowed to grow in her from this individual.

I think GOD for allowing me to come to her rescue, on so many occasions when nobody but GOD could help her in those moments of brutality, sickness, loneliness, depression, fear, and many kinds of attacks from witchcraft bondages. I was honored to help my mother in any way I could. Out of all her twelve children I was the one who had the honor to dress her and make her pretty to meet her maker.

I had the privilege to do her obituary. It was special to me for me to speak for her while she rested in peace. REST IN HEAVENLY PEACE MY DEAR MOTHER. GOD BLESS YOUR SOUL. God is in control of all that concerns you, and me. Don't be deceived God is not mocked. The work he started in you, he will finish if you surrender to his will, and way for your destiny.

The message is God is the potter and we are the clay. Do it God's way or you end up with no way. Simple just like that. He knows the plans he has for you, and the purpose of your being. Let go and let GOD have his way in your heart, mind, and soul. It's the only way to be made whole.

HOW I MADE IT...

Chapter 6

Married Life, And the Drama.

It all started inside the IHOP, on the Maryland side of New Hampshire Avenue. December 6th, 2005, Mister Forbes and I were at this place having breakfast just the two of us. We're eating our food and talking when out of nowhere he asked me to marry him. Wow I knew he wasn't joking, because prior to this day the Holy Spirit put my body on shutdown from him for 30 days no sex. He tried and tried I didn't give in to his temptations the Lord told me no fornicating. If he wants me, he will have to marry me. Well low and behold I didn't think it was coming like this. Although I was very happy, and of course I said yes. Instantly he got on his phone, and called his mother, and told her momma I'm going to marry Tanya. This was another time in my life I was a very happy woman in my heart. In my mind I'm like it's about time, but all at the same time I was grateful I listened to the Holy Spirit when he told me to shut my body down.

The Mister Thought that I was tripping, and hoping that I would give in. Nope I stood my ground, no sex, don't touch me, and I shell not touch you either. When GOD spoke to me it's like he put my hormone side to sleep. I didn't even get hot and horny anymore. So, for me it was easy.

Now get ready this chapter right here is going to be different. I have time and date for a lot of this marriage life. So put your seatbelt on and the roller coaster is about to take off. As I write this, I'm reliving it just remembering the rough pass I've passed through.

December 5th 2005 10:10 a.m. today we thought we were getting married I woke up call my little brother to see if he was going to be a witness at the wedding he said yes call Miss Julie the landlord she had some people coming over this morning to fix the toilet well they didn't come until 5:30 me and the mister read the Bible together play together and I took my oldest son to school who is Devan I got back home to get ready for my marriage me and the mister gets ready and he drives us to the courthouse in Alexandria Virginia on the way there the mister gets into a car accident the police come on the scene and he lets me. Go before releasing him from the scene the police officer gives Mister job to do at his house unbelievable right that's what I'm like okay you just had an accident and the police gives you a side job for him wow okay we still on our way to the courthouse by the time we reach there it's too late no marriage for us I was so disappointed by this we go back home and Mister says we try it again tomorrow that night.

December 6th 2005 11:15 a.m. well this day was the big day Tanya and the Mister are now one my girlfriend Charice came over watch me and the mister get ready for this wedding she even took pictures before we left to go on the road well we got down there they still sent us back home because we had to get the misters passport due to his date of birth not met on his ID we had to go all the way to Baltimore to get his passport I'm doing the driving now and I'm driving like a bat out of hell doing over a hundred miles per hour we made it back to the courthouse just in time once we got there we had to go to another place to do the marriage well we did it we're now one me, and the mister went to get something to eat, and the first person I called was my dad he answer this phone I told him I got married to the Mister from there I went to go see my mom she was happy for us, in her house at the time with my sister Galley, she was mad and didn't speak to me or him we left, and went home to see the children.

My girlfriend Charice came back over for her children could see me and the mister. However, we stepped out to pick up food for the children. After feeding the children the Mister wanted to go have some drinks over his friend's house. We got over Shelton's house to celebrate our wedding. We left from there and went to Michael's another one of his friends' houses. When we arrived at Michael's house, we chill for about an hour and left to go out to eat then back home for me I had a blessed day.

December 7th 2005 11:25 a.m. mind you the time is when I started writing what happening today so I took the white Vans to drop my son off to school then I stopped at the store to pick up groceries for the house. We arrived home and cooked breakfast for the Mister and I. I made his coffee and we ate breakfast together. After eating it's now time for him to meditate, so he goes in the living room and I go upstairs to read my Bible. Before, I can start reading my Bible my phone starts ringing, first it's girlfriend Charice and then my Godmother Becky. Once I ended the call with my Godmother my Brother Hilton called so I let Mister know. The Mister needed Hilton to rent a car, so we picked him up. The Mister gave Hilton $100, and some green. We went back to my house I cooked and gave Hilton an extra plate to take with him before we dropped him back off. Everything went ok this day.

December 4, 2005, I went to church service this particular night with my little brother Donavan, the Mister's children, and my own three children. I let the pastor know this night that we were getting married. Of course, he didn't agree with our decision. He told me to bring the Mister to church, and he will tell me yay or nay. In my mind it was already done. On this day Mister took me to the mall to buy our wedding rings, and clothes. Once I got back home, I had to turn into the barbershop for his son, and mines. Also, I had to cook dinner before it got too late. I remember at the Mall Mister said to me Tanya don't tell anyone we were getting married. I was thinking he's trying to hide me from people. I still told his son when I was cutting his hair, I also showed him my ring. All so he can go back and tell his mother.

Okay I got one that takes us back a month before November 29,2005 11:05am. During this time in Mister's life money is running well, and us women in his life are doing our best to do whatever it takes to stay by his side. The two other baby mothers are fighting over him, with witchcraft curses against each other. He was aware of it but tried his best to tend to his children. So, this night me, and the Mister had a very serious talk about everything, and everybody in his circle. After the talk we went and brought food from the carryout. We went home, ate, and had our showers then went straight to sleep. I was woken up in the middle of the night by the Mister.

Making loud noises and moving very fast up and down on the bed. His body was going through convolutions in his sleep. It was a demon Spirit on him to live and in color for my eyes to see it. I watch them carry on until I heard in my spirit to hit his forehead in the name of Jesus. I slap the mess out of his head in the name of Jesus. I thought he was going to pop up and slap me back, he didn't. However, it woke him up. I cut the light on quickly and sat back on the bed beside him and said, okay let's talk about this what just happened to you. I said you can't say you don't know because you know well and clear you were going through. You were out of control until I hit you out of it. He said he was fighting demons they were trying to kill him. We stayed up until 4:30 a.m. after all this later that morning he gets to call from one of his frenemies Larry.

Mister Larry and Mister started arguing over some money I told the Mister to get off the phone it's nothing but pure confusion coming from him so he got off the call we had moved to make this morning before we left the house need the mister and the children said our prayers together before we all went our separate ways we drop the children off and went on a move I had keys made I had an appointment at Housing, by the time I get there the place was too pack.

I left we went to get something to eat and after went to the nail salon to get a manicure, and pedicure for the both of us. We got our services done and headed back home. On the ride I told him I don't take our conversation last night lightly it's very serious I also asked him so when is the day you plan to marry me he said very soon I said to him if not move out of my life so God can send someone else I was believing that it was going to work out besides I love them so much in my mind I wasn't going anywhere for real I was just tired of the back and forth for so many years I also knew with me having God in my life all things are possible for me.

December 15th 2005 9:30 p.m. well today was the day we're on our way to Florida for a wedding reception the children, Mister and I. The Mister had two vehicles at the time and the Holy Spirit told me to tell him don't drive to Florida, but no Mister wants to save money and didn't want to listen to me and God. He was determined we were riding in his van, so he tells me to get the children and we helped him putting all the bags in the van so we're on our way to Mister's mom house in Davie, Florida. I left my brother Hilton at my house while I was gone on this trip before leaving he stopped at my spiritual mom's house to get prayer and to see if there was a word all mommy told me was it's well and you're going to the next level whatever that meant so we hit the road from there we drove to South of the Border by 2 a.m. and then we parked and went to sleep for a while.

December 16th 2005 at 10 a.m. we got back on the road stopped at the Waffle House to get breakfast and then straight back on the road that Mister did all the driving now it's time for me to take over I'm driving us through South Carolina and Georgia 3 p.m. we're at the side of the road because the car stopped and needed some transmission fluid. So now all me and the children can do is pray. Mister got the hood to the van up, my energy immediately shifted to anger like you mean to tell me you didn't get this van service before putting me and my children in this joint okay trying to stay calm and start singing my gospel and preparing the children it's praying time real talk.

We only left with a certain amount of money getting this van fixed is going to cost us but the Mister have stashed money at the house in the closet. I had to call my mom and my little brother Donovan to go take the money out the safe and send it to us overnight. The money was to meet us down here by the next business day because they FedEx it overnight to his mom's address. Two Thousand was on the way through the mail, because this man didn't want to listen, mind you we're still on the side of the road on no man's land.

We don't know anybody down here to call and ask for help. I started praying and thanks to GOD he sent me an angel named Mister James. Mister James was a white man. He paid for us to get the car towed to the nearest gas station, plus he gave us a ride to the house. None of Mister's relatives were coming to get us, still they all were there waiting on our arrival. So, this so-called reception can take place. When we arrived in front of his mom's house, I saw plenty of cars and trucks. I saw a Mercedes-Benz, Cadillac, and all kinds of fly cars were parked in and around his mom's house. I said to the Mister "you said nobody can come and get us wow." So when we thanked Mister James, got all his information and gave him ours. He left at this point I need a jay yes small weed ASAP. I'm scared, pissed off and trying not to start a fight with the Mister because it's our wedding reception.

You are talking about holding my peace. Oh, so we went inside this fake gathering, and people came from everywhere just to see me, and my three children looking all in my face, and said okay come on y 'all get dressed so this can get started. I looked at Mister, and said we need to talk outside. Mister and I left the house and went on the porch. I said to him "if you don't get me a jay now before I flick off on somebody for not coming to pick us up."

He tells me to stay outside while he goes inside to find me a jay. The children stuck together torn down they were happy to be off the road. The house was flooded good with Jamaican food I must say it was like a buffet, but I didn't care about during that moment. I need to calm down, this was a bit too much and God told his ignorant butt not to drive none of his vehicles from Rent-A-Car.

I know he didn't want to listen so I'm on the porch taking my sweet time smoking, same way they waited for us to get here keep waiting until I come down is what I was thinking. I finally calm down off the influence of the weed. I decided to get the children and myself dressed, so that the reception can begin. We had a pastor there to bless the Lord, people of his family and friends. The big wedding cake was nasty. We chatted together he fed me, and I fed him, you know how it goes. The party didn't finish to early in the morning it was nice, but I had been frustrated by the car, so it took a while for me to watch online got to the tail point though thank God. First thing in the morning, we wake up. On the list of needs is to work on the car. The money came in the morning from FedEx. God is faithful, Mister goes to look at for mechanic I'm staying put with my babies. Go with one of your male family members is what I told him. That's what he did. He ended up putting the car in the shop. It took three days to fix. We were at his mother's house longer than we planned. Oh Lord! Well I'm just going to say after the second day of us being there I went to his mom's room to say goodnight and before I entered the room I heard her on the phone saying I can't wait for them to leave immediately. I went to Mister's room and said she can't wait for us to leave and I can't wait to leave either so that makes two of us not to mention she opened up her door and let out my chihuahua into her neighborhood. My children and I went door to door knocking looking for her but no luck she was confiscated fast. I began to stress Mister about getting me and my children home now. so he went to the mechanic shop to see how much longer the wait was on the van we ended up leaving not much longer after I believe we had another day to stay I'm back on the road to home we was going set alarm.

December 19th on five 10:55p.m. today was the worst day of my marriage with Miss with the Lister Sun this morning mind you we're still at his mom's house in Florida haven't left yet so Mister leaves me and the children in the house while he goes with his friends to fix on the van I was in the house cooking breakfast for the children, and while in the house the phone rang it was the Misters baby mom calling to speak with the Mister. I told her he wasn't available. His kid's mom kept calling back and sending threats through the phone, so I hung up on her. She would call back to back now asking to speak to his mom. I told her she wasn't available either. She cussed and hung up the phone why the mister was gone, I'm on the phone talking to my girlfriend.

The kid's mom kept calling, sending rude threats and messages. I didn't pay her any attention. Hours have passed and the mister comes back after like he got an attitude with me mind you I didn't do anything so take messages and say he wasn't available and which he wasn't so we all the way in Daytona Beach he think we're going to act like fools nope not me he's going to perform by himself. I'm just trying to get back home safe. I asked him that morning to put his armor on, but he didn't like to listen, later that evening he gets mad at me because he wants me to take a ride with him. He didn't put his armor on, so I didn't get in the car with him, but he insist I get in the car. I told him I'm driving then he lets me drive soon as I started to drive, he starts telling me what to do like I don't know how to drive. I yelled at him stop getting on my damn nerves. I pull us into the gas station he gets out to get the gas while he's doing that I'm trying to calm down and humble myself, so I can take him where he needs to go. Low and behold my spirit tells me he's going to call his kids mom. He claims he needs a cigarette, so he walks away from the car to smoke and make his phone call. My spirit was right he's on the phone with his kid's mom. Now I'm upset but I'll wait until the secret is finished before I approached him I say okay let's keep it moving where you had to go now at this time he's closing the conversation with her, I'm so tired of him acting like she's always calling about the kids when in fact it's her just being nosey trying to control him from her end.

However, December 16th to 24th 2005 we went to Florida to do the wedding ceremony, visit his mom and family the road trip we broke down due to him not listening. We had very bad experience with Satan in his mom's house losing a dog. Also, especially a lot of faithfulness and a lot of wanting us to leave. The adults were doing a lot of nitpicking with my children trying to get them into trouble expecting me to beat them, nope not at all, not on y'all watch. I didn't even want to go back.

The wedding ceremony at my church Warriors for Christ was December 24th, 2005 at 3 p.m. I had three of my girlfriends at the church with me as my witnesses along with the Mister's children, and my three children. Girlfriend number 1 was hating out of jealousy. Girlfriend number 2 she was crying out of happiness for me, the other girlfriend was neutral. It was nice that some of my husband's children danced and singed for the wedding. I had to get myself together. His daughter did a holy day dance, it was beautiful. We're all going back home to my house, his four children and my three children, which all on me due to his kids Mom leaving to go to Jamaica after she heard we were getting married. I got to play it by ear because it looks like I'm the babysitter for how long I don't know yet while I'm back getting my neighbors coming over telling me how my brothers had a lot of traffic in and out of my house while I was in Florida. I also found out that both brothers got locked up while I was away. I was grateful for the report at least I had others watching my house I didn't even know about.

December 28th, 2005 6:20 p.m. well the list it takes all the kids to the movies I'm so happy to be left alone now it's time I can pray. The marriage to the Mister been nothing but pure hell. I'm tired of arguing I'm tired of trying to keep our relationship together. I'm tired of taking care of other people's children. It seems like every time I would try to talk to them in a civilized manner he always gets upset and wants to fight. It's not my blood anymore, he shows how he feels when he disrespects me in words or in his actions.

I said to the Lord, I need you to do whatever you're going to do with the both of us, because he has violated me too much at this point. Along with taking my kindness for weakness. This dude really had me cussing him out on this day. He tried to take my sons with him on a drug move. I almost really took his head off that night. Enough is enough, I just can't take him anymore.

January 3rd 2006 10:42 a.m. On this day all his kids got to leave my house immediately. I caught his son trying to have sex with my little cousin's daughter. I've beat his son and my son for watching it and laughing. I called Mister and told him to come and get his kids back to their mom. I said, "if you can't find her I don't care get them out of my house." I feel like he was trying to use me any way he could. I will ask for my bill money and don't worry about the rest God is in control.

 November 12th 2006 2:50 a.m. today I called his phone and had my mom called his phone and let him know I needed money for food and gas money for my car. The Mister didn't answer none of my calls, but he answers the one for my mom, with me on the three-way. He claimed he didn't have any money, so I got feed up and decided ok to let me go find this man, and get what I need for me, and my children. I thanked my mom for calling him, but now it's time for me to go and find him personally. The Holy Spirit told me before I left to take my daughter with me. I tell my daughter to get dressed we're going to find Dad. I ended up at his baby mom's house. The Holy Spirit led me there, I didn't have a clue as to where I was driving all I knew is that once there the Holy Spirit said to me "your here". I began to beep the horn nonstop until I saw the mister come running out the door. I pulled my window down, and I asked him for some money. He pulled out all twenty's and gave me a hundred dollars and said to me ok leave from here fast. Suddenly, a Spirit came over me, it's like I couldn't move. It's like a ton of bricks just laid on me, and I was stuck. I didn't move, and guess who comes out the apartment with pepper spray in her hand hiding under her sleeve the baby mom.

She comes to my side of my jeep. I asked her what do you want bitch? You don't want it. From that she began to spray the pepper spray into the jeep. I hurried up and faced it turning my back to my daughter making sure she didn't get hit with it. The mister was right there watching all of this, not saying anything or stopping anything. I jumped out of the jeep to fight her, and he began to cover her up with his body. I jumped back into the jeep, and I put the vehicle in drive, and ran them over like pancakes. Next, I reversed the vehicle, and rolled over them again. Going forward back over them one more time. I heard the Holy Spirit say you're going to lose your vision in 10 minutes. I'm now driving myself to the police station, but the one closest to my house in SE. Once arriving I lost my vision. My daughter had to help me get out the vehicle to take me inside the police station. Once I get into the station, I go straight to the restroom to wash my face. I'm telling the lady police officer what happened as I'm talking to her and washing my face, I hear my maiden name on the walkie talkie that they got a hit and run. I told the officer no need to go out looking. That name your hearing is me, but my husband gave the police my maiden name, so it won't show he's in the wrong place at the wrong time. The officer was telling me to hurry up with my face that I must go to the police station in Northeast Washington DC where the crime scene was, but then I asked to call my sister down to help me. She came, and we went to the other police station to put my report as to what happened. I called the Mister's Mom, and her sister to tell them what had happened. I called and talked to the pastor to tell them what was going on, and from there they prayed for me. This is going to court, and of course the mister is going to give a statement against me with his baby mother. Wrong move if you ask me, anyway I thank God because it could have been worse. I thank God for protecting me, and my daughter.

November 19th 2006 4:25 p.m. a lot went on this day. I got served at my job in Silver Spring Maryland divorce papers. I stayed away from the Mister, and his baby mom. The pastor was exposed at the church for having a baby by one of the church members, not his wife. On this same day, I had to see the Mister to meet him for some money he gave me $400, and he acted like everything was okay. I got a call from my job that some papers were dropped off for me.

This man came around me knowing what I was going to be faced with, and he still gave me my money, and played everything off like he had no clue of what was coming my way from the courts.

I had go to court on Monday November 20th, 2006 and I will not worry about what will happen because I know God is on my side. The Mister is so stupid he's with his daughter trying to make up lies against me for the job. I can't believe all we have been through together that he would turn his back on me but it's all good. I leave him and her to God. Now in the courtroom the Judge heard the Mister's side, his baby mom's side, and my side. The Judge was going to sentence me to 15 years for the hit and run. However, the hand of GOD. What the Judge did was suspend all the 15 years and gave me two years' probation supervised. Along with a two year stay away order from his baby's mother. The judge told me if I was to violate this order by coming back into his courtroom with any issues from the baby's mom, he was locking the both of us up. He also told me to stay away from the Mister for good. I couldn't believe all the things me and the Mister went through together that he would get on the stand and testify against me. This is something he should have never done. Even after all this betrayal me and him stayed in contact and remained frenemies.

He got deported back to Jamaica, and me and all his children and other two baby moms are here left in the USA. God got me. I went to court in February 2011 to answer the call of me and the misters divorce. I finally wanted out for good. Indeed, the divorce went through without him being there. I sent the divorce papers to him in Jamaica by overnight FedEx express so he could sign them. He signed and sent it back. I paid for a return stamp so he wouldn't have any excuses. I'm free! I want you to know I started this journey with this man at my age of fifteen. He was twenty-seven, I was a loyal, faithful, loving, committed, helpmate to this man. On all levels possible. It's so much more I didn't even add, but to God be all the glory. For these stories, because I've died on two occasions with him, and his baby's mom. it was by witchcraft, and a car accident.

My God said not so and set me back to Earth to finish the work he has started in me. God is faithful no matter what you find yourself in, just be real with your God, and he will show you he is real, and the ruler over your life. I give my life to God who is the author, and the finisher of my faith. No weapon formed against me shall prosper God is a keeper in every area of your, and my life but we must surrender, and turn from our Wicked Ways so that he can get his glory for our stories. God bless you all.

HOW I MADE IT....

CHAPTER 7

SWIM or DROWN TIRED OF THE STRUGGLING.

Swim or drown is a chapter in my life, where I had no other choice but to trust my GOD. In every situation I couldn't see my way out, I couldn't see the light of victory in any angle of the matter, I had no choice but to swim or drown. Six months of my life at this stage with my children homeless nowhere to go, no one would take my children in for me, nobody was there.

All I had was GOD, my husband, and my children at this time in my life. We lived in a Hotel for six months. Going from hotel to hotel with the drug money my husband was making at the time no home cooked meals, no baths, go to the laundromat to wash our clothes. Living out our suitcase changing what we had brought with us. Through all the drama and difficulties, I was catching hell from the devil. I had to remain humble. I couldn't afford this husband of mine to abandon me and the children at this time. I finally found a house for rent on Westover Drive. S.E This house was a huge blessing for me because it was fully furnished. All we had to do was move in with our clothes. I came up with the first month's security deposit and the rent. Moving in time was easy. I lived in this house for 5 years. Good and bad moments were remembered here. No matter what the enemy tried to do to bring chaos in my life God has been my restorer and my personal deliverer.

I remember the first time I gave in to my dad to let him come over and see how the Lord has been taking care of me and my children. He talked to us for a bit of time then before leaving he asked to use the bathroom. Me not knowing how the bathroom is the secret place to say and do things. I let him go without any thought process. Well this was on Friday night. Saturday came and my family household was upside down arguing with each other, fighting and nothing but pure confusion.

When Sunday came, I took me and my children to church. I prayed to Abba Father what had happened to me and my children. The Holy Spirit showed me in prayer that my dad had dropped something in my bathroom, it told me to clean my bathroom out with bleach and sweep it out good. Then the Holy Spirit told me to get all of my children and we had to anoint the whole house with holy oil and spray holy water in every room for me to command that evil spirit to go out of my house and send them to the red sea never to return back again. Me and my children did just that the peace of God came back into my home. It's amazing how the enemy would always try to destroy me, and my children but God wouldn't leave us in the pit of confusion and the illusions.

I remembered being locked up over DC Jail for 6 months on a warrant that was out for my arrest. While there the Lord came to visit me in my cell. The Lord came to me while I was laying down and said to me, I will get you out of this, but you must serve me all the days of your life in good times and in bad times. I told the Lord I will do just that. It was a relief to me because I know after this my day of being released was coming soon.

Swim or Drown,

Seven days in the George Washington Hospital. I went in because of my stomach hurting and pain in my right side. When I got there, they took my blood, hooked me up to IV and started running the test. I began getting hot and cold chills next a fever came, before I knew it I was being admitted. I remember my two daughters came with me once I was being admitted.

The nurses said my daughters had to leave. I told them if they leave, I leave. I didn't have anyone to keep them, mind you my daughter is 23 at the time and my next daughter was 4 they both had to stay with me in this hospital.

Once we realized I wasn't going back home and the coast was clear we set the atmosphere in the room I was staying in, we began to pray and call the Holy Spirit down. The Lord told me to put some music on but no words, so they won't know who you are. I went to my pandora and put on spiritual instrumentals no words only pleasant sounds we were praying and asking God for war angles to come and stay watch over us in this room. By 12 midnight a witch nurse came to give me medicine. I refused it and she called for another nurse to work with me. When she left I binded her up and commanded her assignment with me canceled and sent to the pits of hell. I covered this whole room and me and my daughters with the blood of Jesus Christ. As days went by, I was taking medicine for my pain while they were trying to find out what was wrong with me. Well as I was in this hospital the Lord revealed to me this was a bow and arrow from the witches of my bloodline. I was working at the nursing home at this time. They were mad at me because I was going around praying and healing for the people.

Out of nowhere they hit me with two sicknesses trying to get me out of the job. By this time, they have tried to do so many things to make me leave or get fired by their traps and lies but not one of them worked. I was covered by the blood of Jesus Christ; they couldn't stop me. It was a sad 6 months of no pay, no work hours they thought I was going to quit. Nope I kept coming to have meetings with the administrators to see why I was off the schedule without reason. No one could answer only to say it's still under investigation. Now, back to the hospital. The Chief Doctor for disease came in and wanted me to sign off on him going deeper to cut my insides open to see what they could see.

I prayed about it. The Lord told me to tell him no, it's nothing there, it's all an attack from the enemy, don't let them use you as a guinea pig. The Doctor said he wanted to give me a few more drugs to decide. I decided right then and there you're not cutting me period.

Different head Doctors would try to convince me this might be another way they can check deeper to see if I had an infection inside. By what they see so far, all my tests came back negative. I kept praying everyday trusting in God when he was going to release me from this place. I didn't give in and I kept taking pain meds eventually the attack left me. On day seven the Chief Doctor of disease came into my room telling me he had to respect my choice, but my insurance won't hold me any longer.

That's if I choose for them to go in would I come back to the hospital to let them do the test. I told him sure just to get him out of my face and release me. He did just that I was being released the next day. This was a death arrow that was thrown at me from the witch's cover, but the blood of Jesus Christ never lost a patient. God is faithful, he is a healer and redeemer it was only God that kept me and made me back to normal.

After being discharged the next day the Lord told me to go get all my records out of that hospital before they try to use it against me years later. I went to the records department and requested for all my records while I was there for that week. I had to pay for them plus wait for them to be delivered to my house but they came. Thank you, Lord, for keeping me when I couldn't explain or understand how to keep myself. Holy Spirit was my guide every step of the way. The sickness and death arrow went back to sender; it didn't conquer me at all.

Swim or drown,

I went back to work fought it until one day in December the Lord said that's it go apply for unemployment. Once the case was under investigation the people in the HR department tried to deny my unemployment with lies. Thanks to God, they found out they were lying on me and approved my case in spite of the denial from my past employer. God is a faithful God. I worked that job for 6 years. I was pushed out because I was too good, too kind and too honest. Oh well God kept me through this too.

Swim or drown,

However, being in the house no food, no money, I saw it coming as the days would pass. I was cooking making miracle meals out of what little bit of food that was left in the house. I prayed, went to church and came back home one of my girlfriends called me and said God put me in her heart. Once I told her my situation, she began to put food together out of her refrigerator, packed some bags and paid for an uber for my daughter to bring it back home. This was well appreciated.

I didn't know who or where the food was coming from. I just trusted God to move. Also, while the night was growing closer the devil wanted me to doubt God. Nope I fixed my children some Noodles and for myself I wasn't hungry I was fasting, so I didn't care about the food. That call was right on time and it was enough food to hold us over until my pay day came. Swim or drown. I remembered I cooked the last meal this particular night. I told my children this is the last of it until God moves again. Now this time is a week before Christmas.

 Thank God my oldest children weren't tripping off Christmas, but I still had my little girl who for me was still young, so she really didn't know. Although my oldest kept putting in my head ma you made sure we had a Christmas it's only right for her to have one too. I began to seek the Lord about the next meal I would feed my children. Forget about Christmas on my mind at this time. I need to make sure my baby doesn't experience hunger pains in her belly due to me not feeding her. I prayed and cried out to God, I felt like just laying down and going to sleep. It's out of my hands at this time.

Once I prayed, I left it with the Lord, with no doubts of him working another miracle for me. How, what, when, and where I have no clue, So I lay down in my son's bed. I dozed off and woke back up and i heard the Lord say call your big sister, I called her, and she was apologetic for not having nothing of any money to give me. I wasn't even mad I just was shocked I heard God say her and she didn't have anything for me. Next as i get off the phone with her I hear the spirit say to me don't be mad at her. So, I just hung up the phone and laid back down.

Next the Lord spoke again, and he told me to call this lady. She is an African, I called her and told her my situation as she was trying to rush me off the phone. The spirit said to tell her quickly you don't have nothing, no food or money to feed your children. I hurried up and said it. Before she got off the phone, she said go check your cash app I sent you something, I said ok and hung up the phone. I went to my cash app and once I saw $500.00, I screamed thank you Jesus Christ. I fell on my knees and began to praise God thanking him for yet another miracle for me and my children as I was on the floor thinking about my daddy Abba Father. I heard the spirit say to me go to your son, and show him what I can do, for him to trust me in everything no matter how big or small trust God, and he will provide for you. All I could do is cry to God thanking him for always making a way for me out of no way. Remember to cast all your cares on God. He will provide for you because he cares for you.

Swim or Drown

You will have moments in life where you feel just like this swimming sometimes and other times you're feeling like you're drawing in your sin, in your displacement, in your doubt, in your fears, in your sickness, in your stressful not knowing how change is going to come. It's then when I want to encourage you to stay focused, don't give up. Don't give in to trust God when you don't have anything to trust. Other than your breath that you're breathing I'm sure you know it's not on your own will nothing is happening. Trust God no matter how low you find yourself. Trust God no matter how many accomplishments you established, Trust God when you can't see him or hear him.

You will swim in the world with the help of God or you will drown if you allow the devil to take you for his faithless ride, beliefs, doubts, attacks, sickness, mental illness, hurt, pain, and unforgiveness. You chose will you swim or will you drown. It starts with you and will end with the choices you free willingly decide to do. Don't blame God for your outcome he gave all free will. You choose blessings or you choose curses.

Swim or Drown, this is a time you must have all your faith, trust and assurance in the Lord God. When your own children revolt against you. You put time, love, money, patients, teachings, trust into these once as babies now adults to hope and pray one day they will be mighty men and women living in the fear of God first and then to live a life as the way God planned for them through their own life teachings and experience. On the flip side I thank God for keeping and teaching me how to be a parent.

I thank God for forgiving me when I always thought violence was the answer to every wrong to make it right. When the children would get into trouble or would disrespect me. I want to say raising a family by myself has been a swim or drown moment. Through the tough times, hard to make ends meet times, times when I didn't have a place for them to lay their heads, times when i didn't know where the next meal was coming from, or i didn't know how I was going to cloth them, this had really been a swim or drown moment.

 Times when you must teach them the fear of God, the morals, and respect for themselves, each other, and for others. Swim or drown when all else fails God never failed me or my children so i just write this to encourage someone that God is faithful in all areas of your life if you trust him and surrender your will to his will everyday you have to die to your flesh and let the will of the father take control. He's a keeper, a provider, a protector, a doctor, a lawyer, a way out of no way you decide whether you swim or drown.

Working in Cedar Hill Cemetery was a dark depression moment, everyday before I could enter this building I had to buy me fresh flowers for my desk. The darkness and the death spirit that flooded this place was very heavy. I prayed everyday even throughout the day of being on this ground of death. God was my peace, my protection from the unseen spirits of darkness. I couldn't concentrate in this place of darkness. I didn't make any sales. My focus was keeping my eyes on God as learning how to prepare for that last day. I didn't work here long. I learned what I needed to do and got out. God moved me,

(***Swim or Drown.***)

HOW I MADE IT....

CHAPTER 8:
HOLDING ON LETTING GO AND LETTING GOD

After dying four times and being brought back to life. NOTHING! but the Spirit of the living God kept me alive. After being stabbed, guns pulled on me, getting beat by a gun, being raped, after being homeless, having no food, no shelter, no friends and no family, Felling the rejection made me strong. The hurt, and pain in this life has been a learning experience. Even in my darkest moments I can see God's hands on me and all around me, keeping me from losing my mind, keeping me from jail, betrayal and Crime.

In every season of my life from 12 years old till 45 years old I never let go of God's hand I never stopped trusting him, I never stopped having faith that no matter what the situation is, I still know that God is in control, and he will answer by Fire. I'm not perfect, I will never be, but I serve a perfect God who's in control of my everyday life, and everybody around me. So, my faith will never leave me knowing God has the final say over everything that concerns me. I'm letting go, and letting God, for he is good, and his mercy endures forever.

When something is given to you and then taken back, let go and let God, when someone you think loves you or has your best interest and gives you something you take it , not knowing one day they will say, well it's not your or that they want it back. It is not your place to say yes or no. If the person wants to allow the devil to use them to take back what they have given you, that means they never really wanted you to have it.

Let them have it back in a loving manner and let it go, but never expect anything else from them or that spirit. it's a confused spirit it's not sure who it's serving so be confident in the gift of giving. Always keep serving God no matter good or bad. The Lord will change things and bless you with blessings that won't be taken back or bring sorrow. God will make a new way for you, just trust him in whatever situation you're in, letting go and letting God. When you're a child of the King Lord Jesus, people will see the light in you and will hate you because of what they see you. I'm not here to make people's day go great. I'm just a servant of God. In being a child of the Lord Jesus, people will try and cause all types of grief and strife, and guess what all just for spite. Well I love everyone because the Lord requires me to.

Believe me it's hard to love people who hate you, mistreat you, use and abuse you every way that they know how to. They will even lie on you, so they do what they must do by the influence of the devil, against you. Remember no weapon formed against you shall prosper if you only believe. Things happen to you in your life so you can open your eyes to see who's there for you, and to see who's never going to leave you. Don't get it confused its only good people who will never leave you nor forsake you. God allows it to happen so you can decide who to trust and believe. When you are letting go and letting God there's no good thing will he withhold from you. Don't put your trust in humans only in God. He's the only one who can take the pain, shame, anger and turn it into love, patience, peace, and justice for your good. Letting go and letting God take the contacts out of your eyes so you can see naturally, and spiritually.

Take the sin out of your life so you can grow spiritually rooted and grounded in God's work the way he ordained you to be. When you Let go and let God, who will you end up being?

A student who goes to school, everyday trying your best to be the smartest in your class, or a student who don't pay attention, don't listen, don't do anything they supposed to. Who else will you end up being? A drug dealer in the streets, stacking money till you're caught up in the game of fame, not acting the same. Always with fresh new things, before you know it, you will be in the cell wishing like hell you can smell some home cooked food.

Where will you end up being? A Nurse in the nursing home, changing the pampers, or whipping the slob of the older folks, changing the bed, feeding them while holding their head, washing the clothes, and making them smile for the little while of your shift. What will you end up being? A Professor at Howard University, studying and protesting about black power, what will you end up being? A Newscaster, catching all the drama, studying weather, crimes, politics, stocks and bonds, don't forget about being an advocate for the government, and reporting about people who are sick with plagues and pestilence, every season for no reason. No love, no respect, no motivation only to receive a check. People are waiting on the next doctor's visit, or welfare check to be another suspect. However, will you let go and let God be in you who he has made you to be? Romans 11:36 "God created everything of him and through him and to him are all things to whom be glory forever." AMEN!

Letting go and letting God when you allow the heavenly father to be in total control of your life, there's a peace that is in you, and a positive influence that will guide you. You must pray and ask for direction of the simplest and the most difficult decision to make sure you're going in the right direction when letting go and letting God. You must always use discernment in every area so as you keep your faith, trusting in God over the situation. You will not be fooled by the false prophets and people who know the word of God, and still have the audacity to use it for their self-material gain.

Letting go and letting God doesn't mean be a fool for the mockery of God from man or female. Letting go, and letting God means to purify yourself by getting rid of fear, letting go of anger, letting go of envy, letting go of lying, letting go jealousy, letting go of covetousness, letting go of pride, letting go of hatred, letting go of worldliness, letting go of drug use, letting go of drinking alcohol and strong drinks, letting go of rebellion against God's purpose and plan for your life, letting go of all distractions operating under demonic influence once you do this you will be made whole.

God will use you for his divine purpose as you read the word of God and die to your flesh daily of your everyday living. In life you must have a solid foundation to build and only what you do for Christ will last. Holding on to the word of God letting the word of God become your daily routine before starting your day, your holding on to God with faith in all you have left. Putting all your trust in God is not foolish, putting your trust in God holding on the foundation to beginning and the end, in that you won't go wrong.

God is the first and the last of all mankind he gives life, and he takes life. Keep holding on to God's unchanging hand he is the same yesterday today and tomorrow. I'm holding on to the foundation of my faith in God through his son Jesus Christ. I encourage you to keep holding on to your faith in the good times, in bad times, in sick times, in unsure times. Trust God, in waiting and it's taking a long time to see an answer or a change don't give up, don't give in, keep your faith and be faithful keeping yourself pure and you will definitely receive your answer from God in ways you least expect him to show up.

Sometimes we must encourage ourselves that it's going to be okay, things are going to get better even in a failing moment, in a loss of a loved one don't lose hope for the love and trust you have in God.

Letting go and letting God can mean so many things from different perspectives at this point in my life I'm allowing God through the Holy Spirit to lead, guide and direct my paths in this life. I'm content to a degree in all at the same time I'm not anxious for nothing. If it's meant to be, it will be. We can have all the dreams and goals but if it's not in God's plan for you or me to have it, it will be done. You will make yourself overwhelmed when you're operating out of the will of God.

We must speak the blood of Jesus Christ over our lives every day. We must be consistent in our morning devotion with God and the Holy Spirit in the lives of those who are around us. We must pray and allow the will of God to take control of the individual. Move all feelings and emotions aside, just intercede on their behalf that God will adjust and make the person live in the fear of God. Living a righteous life, having a spirit of discernment as much as possible in every area of life. Only what you do for God will last. Letting go of flesh desires will allow the flow of the Holy Spirit to guide you in your destiny without the distractions of the adversary. Get prepared, the time will come that it's good against evil, try your best to do good over evil. It's very hard at times but it can be done with much discipline and self-control.

However, you must be used by the Holy Spirit walking and living in the Holy Spirit, and not in the flesh. Die to the flesh daily. Don't let the adversary use you to commit the acts of evil through anger, rage, arguing, fighting, cursing, speaking evil, and wishing evil. Stay calm in all areas. Irritation and losing patience with a person or situation are real. Find ways to let the energy go by without demonic activity.

Pray always without ceasing, keep your spirit pure so you can be available when God may need you to intercede on his behalf. Keeping yourself pure by purifying your spirit by letting go of fear, vanity, anger, envy, lying, malice, covetousness, lust, pride, hatred, and all forms of worldliness. When in weakness the spirit is made strong through God, and the Holy Spirit. You can't serve two masters; you must love one and despise the other. God will always out live the evil. Leave all vengeance to God to repay your enemies. As you're holding on letting go and letting God, he will perfect that which concerns you on a daily basis of life.

 Living in the fear of the Lord, Alpha and Omega, don't forget not to lose your faith in God. Please trust God with all your heart, soul and mind. Even when things don't look like it's working in your favor. God is in total control and he will direct your path if you only trust and Never lose hope in the creator of the universe who has a purpose for your being on this earth for certain people. Don't think you will be received by everyone it's only the selective that God has picked for you to reach that will receive you and understand you.

Many of the rest will thank you crazy or you're not in the will of God. Those kinds remember if they don't receive you, they don't reject you, but the God that lives in you through the Holy Spirit. Don't try to convince anybody of your elect calling by God. God makes room for the gifts he's placed in you to use effectively through the leading of the Holy Spirit. In the process of holding on don't lose your focus on God. Release your will to the will of God and let go of your desires and let God have his way in your life. God will finish what he has started if you live and respect the laws of the Kingdom and follow all his Ten Commandments.

While time and life will change and get more and more challenging, remember God is the creator of all things, he will make a way out of no way, God is faithful. Be very careful of the words you speak out of your mouth. I had to learn to speak things that weren't as though they were. It sounds backwards but it works in the same aspect: listen to people's words closely if it's not something good and in the will of God bind it up in Jesus Christ name that it won't travel and take effect on your situation. Letting go and letting God. Stay sensitive to the Holy Spirit when you're feeling irritated and just frustrated. Plead the blood of Jesus Christ over your life and situations so it may change and keep the devices of the devil away and off you.

Remember to commit your spirit to the spirit of the living God in Christ Jesus. Stay humble and be able to handle rejection from all walks of life. Be able to handle humility. Keep the pride full spirit away, don't look down on nobody. Help and gift to others as much as the Spirit of God makes it available for you. You never know how God would return the favor by the works and deeds you have done to his people. Store up your treasures in heaven, only what you do for Christ will last. Don't do anything looking for a return by no human. Do everything out of your heart and know that God of this universe will reward you accordingly. He promised to supply all your needs according to his riches in glory.

HOW I MADE IT....

Chapter 9 Religion:
Dealing with My life, My Faith, and Witchcraft from my Enemies.

    I believe in Jesus Christ, my Savior, and my redeemer. I believe my job is to convert and win souls for the Kingdom of God. Not having no debates but giving the sinner a chance to admit being a sinner and accepting Jesus Christ as Lord, over one's life. Confessing and surrendering the spirit to the will of God through his son Jesus Christ. There are many religions and a lot of different kinds of beliefs in this world. The only one I know of having power and proving it by actions and deeds are Jesus Christ the son of God. Once you confess out of your mouth that you are a sinner and you believe that Jesus Christ died for your sins, and you want him to come into your heart to take full control of your life you then become one of the sons and daughters of Jesus Christ. No man could come to the father except by the son.

Many challenges will come to test you, as well as mold you into the purpose driven spirit God has advanced you to be originally. I believe every human being has a purpose in this world. Not everybody is here to be living under the control of the Holy Spirit. Some are here to carry out the works in the plans of Satan. You must keep yourself, and family clear of those types of people. They have nothing to lose especially if they have sold their soul for something.

Once that action is done, they begin to recruit people to make them come into their cult, or demonic organization, by many common pressures and initiations of many kinds. Fear is a major tactic the enemy will use to make you join him in his demonic actions and attempts. If your spirit is not covered by a spiritual covering, it's easy for the enemy to enter the mind of the individual and begin to speak and show a lot of false promises. The enemy will say a lot of hurtful things as well as cause the pain and suffering it's all an illusion for a certain amount of time Which is when God makes the devil take his hands off you if your one of his children, if not the suffering is eternal for the soul of the devil's child.

The father of all lies is the adversary. That spirit called the devil has agents assigned to different people and their family blood line through generational curses that's been sitting for years and generations without being handled. However, nothing was done, and devil has taken so many lives by way of fear and doubt, along with living in the souls without total deliverance from the possessions of the devil.

Religion will make you look over the topic of deliverance. This is done by being in routine of set programs in a long-time religion and by laws. Singing songs, preaching a word, laying of hands with no power, no help from the Holy Spirit. True repentance is the first thing that must be done. Confessing the sins and telling God you're sorry along walking away from it and never to return to that sin. Forgiveness is another one people say and really don't do it. Forgiveness is a must if we want God who is in heaven to forgive us of our sins. Baptism is a must to go with the confession, repentance and forgiveness. Baptism is the only way our sins can be remitted, washed and taken away in the name of Jesus Christ. Once you've repented, you're on the way to being born again. You must have faith in God and your trust must be totally in the one God Alpha and Omega, Abba Father, through his son Jesus Christ.

You must have a relationship with God through his son Jesus, being his disciple and winning souls for God through Christ Jesus. The spirit of the Holy Spirit must be in the lives of the individual that has walked away from their sinful life and actions, to be connected to the body of Yahushua, Jesus Christ. Keeping a clean spirit, stay connected to God through your son Jesus Christ. Read your bible daily, confess your sins regularly, give to the less fortunate, keep your trust in him no matter how low you may go. Keep an open relationship with your Master Jesus Christ. Stay connected to the Holy Spirit don't allow yourself to be disconnected by the people you live with, your job, your parents or any influence that isn't living and doing the will of God through actions as well as confessions. Don't grieve, the Holy Spirit will be your teacher and all things. In reference to God and relating to people. You must have the spirit of the living God living in you. You must separate yourself from the world.

You can live in this world but don't be a part of the wicked worldly daily actions. In order to be born again one must be baptized by water and baptized by the Holy Spirit, by fire. Don't give up the Holy Ghost for a worldly reward. In the Bible John 14:26 "but the comforter which is the Holy Ghost whom the father will send in my name he shall teach you all things and bring all things to your remembrance whatsoever I have said unto you." Hebrews 10:25 "not neglecting our own congregational meetings as some have made a practice of doing, but rather encouraging each other." Let us do this more as you see the days approaching. 1John 2:27, "But the anointing which ye have received of him Abide in you, and ye need not that any man teach you; But as the same anointing teaches you of all things and it's truth and is no lie, and even as he hath taught you. Ye shall abide in him."

Matthew 18:20 for wherever two or three are assembled in my name, I am there with them. Religion stops you from having a relationship with the son of God. We must always maintain an open daily relationship with the Heavenly Father. The enemy will try and weary you out by making you tired, lazy, using procrastination, fear, doubt, and unforgiveness to keep his hand on you or your progress. Read your Bible daily and fast these weapons of warfare will help you get through a lot of stumbling blocks sent your way from the distractions of the devil. Sometimes things happen to you not because you're a bad person, not because your lifestyle isn't a certain way. God is allowing the sin of the father to catch the child. Not only that, trials and tribulations come in many forms, of pain and suffering. As there are many different diversities in life. So, It's same with your religion or the belief of many individuals. God is the creator of all, love is the key to win in trials and tribulations when it comes to involving people.

Work with people from a loving heart. Do things out of love, discipline out of love, correct out of love, teach out of love, encourage faith in a person by the way of love. Have understanding out of love. Defend someone out of love. Change because of love. Love is a game changer. Have patience out of love. Agree to disagree out of love. Give out of love. In any way you can help someone do it out of true genuine love. Be at peace with all people showing love to all that meets you. Talk in love, give good guidance in love. John 3:16 "for God so loved the world that he gave hours only begotten son that whosoever believe in him should not perish but have everlasting life."

Sometimes you must be very careful because who you confide in and put your trust into. It's not everybody you help of love that's going to have your and their best interest. My lessons of being betrayed by close friends, family, loved ones, co-workers, strangers, and church colleagues.

The betrayal and jealousy of those God has been unbelievable for me to even believe. I can't understand how these people can smoke with you, eat with you, work with you, cry with you, make love to you, and still back stab you to your face. Manipulate any situation to their advantage. The forces of darkness are the real reason behind it all. Darkness in this world was made to manipulate, control, and spread darkness of manipulations to humanity for ownership. Ownership of one's soul.

You must be very wise and live a God-fearing life because the adversary who you call the devil only cares to do a few things to mess up a person's belief and confidence in the true creator. He's outs to steal, kill and destroy. Who he uses it is the least of his concerns all he wants is your soul, disconnected from the true and living God? Many distractions will be used to keep your mind confused and fearing to fight, pray and fast for your strength and salvation in Christ. The enemy main objective is to win souls for his kingdom which is hell.

Many things will come in the form of love, opportunity, employment, 2nd career change. One must be in tune with the spirit of the living God into the spiritual realm of God and the universe in order to keep yourself balanced on the right path of destiny designed for you. Be a leader and love from a view of openness to the spirit and soul, owing no human nothing but to love them. Beware of the darkness and the influence of evil manipulations, they are here as well only to gain more souls for the kingdom of darkness by fear, power, wealthiness for a matter of time, and material gain.

The love of money, selfishness and power gain. Beware of cults, and societies, that will want you to exchange your soul for resources and material gain. Having a close relationship with God is very important to both the believer and the neutral person. Having peace of mind is more than having money. Only God can give you a sure peace of mind, dignity from God, assurance from God, and all needs met by God. Only if you put him first, and study well also keeping clean hands and pure hearts.

Following the Ten Commandments taking full accountability of your lifestyle and actions. Repent from your sins. Don't fight against the voice inside of you. There is a small still voice inside of each of us that is God in us. He will always speak first also he will always give you the right guidance. God will not allow the adversary to speak first to his children, don't doubt your inner self. Your consciousness is always awake and working. Ask Adam the Holy Spirit for guidance and answers to whatever you have questions to.

The Holy Spirit reveals everything no matter how big or small it is, you will get an answer if your spirit is in a peaceful place to receive the answer. Peace in your soul and mind, tuning out all nosey distractions so a clear communication can come through for, the voice of the Lord. Don't block out your wisdom and understanding of God. Wisdom will flow through your inspiration, as well as the fear of the Lord are the principles to keeping your communication open to God. All of these you will need to stay clear of all ungodly forces of darkness and sin. Repentance is always needed daily.

Dying to your flesh daily and allowing the Holy Spirit to take control will be needed for your purpose destiny to be fulfilled. Win the battle against your own mind by submitting all your thoughts into God. Casting down all vain imaginations. Choose to live a Godly life so that the will of God will manifest. No matter the test and the trials, you will be living a life pleasing to God and, always having the fear of God. Always make sure you choose to live a Godly life no matter how your being treated or whatever may be happening.

Make sure you're praying without stopping in all areas. Resist all temptations of wickedness, and fleshly desires. Make sure you apply fasting with your daily prayers. As you grow stronger and longer in the will of God, you will need to be equipped to do the full will of God. Engage the word of God in your heart to remind yourself not to sin against the will of God in your life. Try your best to live a God-fearing life well pleasing to God. All these things are needed to live a full pleasing life to yourself and to God.

Don't be disobedient to the will of God for your life, do what God wants you to do. Fear God and have no other Gods before him. Repent and resist the works, distractions, plans and temptations of the devil. Make serving God a priority everyday and you will live a blessed, healthy, happy, peaceful life.

Command your flesh to decrease and allow the Holy Spirit to increase daily in your life.

I've overcome death, sickness, betrayal, incarceration, homelessness, no food, or clothes, joblessness, rejection, and many wicked evil traps from the devil and his workers. Auditions from lust, drugs, and selling drugs, alcohol, and people's opinions, many trials, disappointments and failures but God delivered me from them all. I'm sent to heal the broken hearted, to use my life experiences to help someone else overcome the pains of life that I passed through overcoming the devices of the devil in one's life, through prayer and fasting, deliverance, reading the word of God and giving charity to whoever is in needed at the time. Keep a clean heart and clean hands. Staying watchful of the temptations and worldly manipulations. Praying against everything that will try and move your mind, body soul and spirit out of the will of God. If I told you the walk with God and Jesus Christ is an easy one. I would be lying, in fact it's a steady work, and always trying to your flesh.

Putting on the whole armor of God, commanding your flesh to decrease so the Holy Spirit will increase. Submitting yourself to the will of God. There is a purpose for all mankind. Allow God to deliver you from your sinful ways, be tired of being a slave to the devil and your fleshly desires. True love towards all human beings without selfish desires, or motives reveals the love of God in you for all humanity. Never underestimate your gift strength and encouragement you hold within yourself.

Your positivity, and strength to go on after so many trials, tribulations, downfalls, attacks, sickness, homelessness, friendless, foodless, lifeless, and insecurities from within. Only God the creator has that power to raise you up again. Better than the last time. In life you might have to fall down many times.

You might not understand the full reason why? Just remember you're blessed and a new day in the land of the living is proof you have another chance to win again. Don't give up, don't give in just keep trusting God until the day he calls you in.

No day is the same, not one person is the same we're all different in God's image and likeness. Let his plan and will for your being manifest to change someone in this land of the living. Sometimes you must encourage yourself to remind yourself that things will happen that's out of your control. Things will happen that will make you feel sad, when it's not going the way you expect them to be or go. Sometimes you must endure hardship but be a good person while going through many trials and tribulations for there are many afflictions of the righteous but God Shall deliver you from them all.

Don't try to defend yourself when people lie on you. Don't try to prove yourself to anyone just keep a clean heart, keep your mind stayed on God, do everything from a pure clean heart, be a leader for Christ and not a follower of the devil. Don't be ashamed when you're rejected but people, loved ones, career opportunities and society. You and all people are uniquely made by God, everyone is special to God, he makes no mistakes. The way he brought you into this world is special in God's plan for your purpose and destiny.

Everything works together for the good of them that love the loggers and are called according to his purpose Romans 8:28. John 5:20 for the father loveth the son, and sheet him all things that himself doeth: and he will shew greater works than these, that ye may marvel. So, you see God has your destiny already planned out. Seek God early in the morning, commit yourself and spirit mind and body and soul to the will of God, and ask him to guide you into his plans for your day and life. Denying yourself flesh will help you stay humble in many tough situations that may occur in your daily day.

There will be many test trials, and different types of manipulation you might find yourself involved in as you've committed yourself and spirit into the will of God. The Holy Spirit will work for you when the afflictions of the enemy come to attack you.

Whether it be sickness, car accidents, homelessness, mental, illness, divorce, death of love ones, loss of job, loneliness, rape, molestation, depression, suicidal thoughts, born with deformities, being an orphan, catalyzation, being mute, having seizures, God and hours infinite power can deliver you, help sustain you and allow you to cope with whatever your facing in this life path you're in.

One must have faith and believe in the power of God, and his son Jesus Christ for the power of the Holy Spirit to work in the speaking, leading and teaching of the ways of God. The Holy Spirit is the help of humanity in all areas of life. Without the Holy Spirit it is very difficult for the human race to succeed. For the struggle isn't with flesh, and blood but against principalities, Powers and the rollers of this dark world. The principalities and powers in this world represent the total of evil powers that threaten the faith in human beings both heavenly and earthly. The whole world is run by a force of dark spiritual powers, therefore the fear of God, the faith in God, and trust in God as much needed to survive while living in this world. Don't be deceived God is the creator of heaven and earth.

He is the beginning and the end. He has allowed the fallen angel Lucifer to rule over this earth. After he becomes dissatisfied with his life in hell, he goes around seeking whom he may devour quickly before the return of Jesus Christ.

Keep your soul spirit, mind and body protected by accepting Jesus Christ as your savior, repent daily of all your sins known and unknown. Do your best to give charity, and envy nobody, love yourself and your life. Be a Godly example to all in your circle. Show the love of God to all humanity. God gives free will of the choices you make in this life. Don't leave your spirit uncovered by not having the divine protection of Jesus Christ of Nazareth. Owing no man nothing but to love them except people for who they are, and judge no one. If you can help someone who is less fortunate than you do something from the love of God and Christ Jesus in your heart.

God will reward us all on the day of judgment. Only what you do for Christ will last. Read the word of God, let it minister to your life and apply the Holy Spirit to all your choices and decisions you need to make in life. The helper God left for all who believe won't steer you wrong God is faithful in all things.

HOW I MADE IT......

CHAPTER 10
I'M A SURVIVOR

In my life I've had many bad, difficult, sad, lonely, painful life or death unforgettable afflictions, and situations, that I've overcome only by the hand of God in my life. I'm not proud of all the things I've done in my life. I'm not ashamed of anything I've done or had to do. As I see it was all a part of God's plan that God had for my life. I started out with many so-called friends and associates in my life. I ended up with only one true friend, and that's GOD and his precious Holy Spirit he left with me. The first 46 years of my life has been a li bit of everything for me being, confused, Rejected, frustrated, uncertain, determined, happy, fortunate, strong minded, abandoned, and much perseverance to continue my path called destiny whether delay or denial. I've been determined to allow God to have his way with my life. Along with me adding whatever successfulness I was able to achieve along my way. Running my own race in this life, being my own self-motivation at times.

Encouraging myself with the word of God, trying my best to be the best example of a true believer in God and his son Jesus Christ, whoever comes to know me. My assurance in trusting in God Mentally, physically, and emotionally. Most of all spiritually only came from the touch and love of God's hand in my life. The only way I have been able to overcome all adversities is having, trials, obstacles, failures, disappointments, and rejections, in any form of fashion, sent from the adversary. God has shut the mouth of everyone working and saying evil against my life. Isaiah 54:17 "No weapon formed against me shall prosper and every tongue that rises against me shall be condemned." This is the heritage of the servants of the Lord, and their righteousness is of me, saith the Lord.

I will never forget the moneyless, foodless days and nights, homelessness, sickness, being incarcerated, deaths, failures, betrayals, rejections, abandonments, possessiveness, being misunderstood, and making my way through life. God has been with me through it all, good times and bad times he's been my keeper. This book isn't all of what I've had to overcome, it's just a few things I've decided to share with the world and the people in it, that the creator is so real. You must choose who side you will reside on. God's side or the devils side. It's no in-between, It's either one or the other. God and his son Jesus Christ are life eternal, the devil's side is hell fire and gnashing of teeth. Being on God's side, it keeps you connected to the presence of God and the provision of God and his benefits of God releasing hundreds of blessings into your life. To be with God in Spirit and in truth you will have to suffer many persecutions, trials and tribulations. Count it all joy because when this world is over for you, and it's time to face judgement day, you will be with him in heaven.

I thank God for choosing me to be one of his servants to live by my experiences to show a sinful world of people that we must repent, and be baptized by water, and by fire of the Holy Spirit to represent God the Father, God the son, and God the Holy Spirit. God gives each of us free will, you can choose Blessings or curses. Deuteronomy 28 describes this very clear and plain to all generations. There will be no excuses, on judgement day. My life message is clear: Repent for the kingdom of God is at hand. Except Jesus Christ as your savior, and let the HEALING, leading of the Holy Spirit become your teacher, guidance in all areas of your life.

God is a gentleman through his son Jesus Christ he will not force his will on no one. You are free to choose where you will spend life after death at. I'm sure everyone won't agree with me, and my testimonies. How I made it in the fire without a burn on me. I'm fine with that, I'm only here to help free those that believe in God first, and secondly those that wish to be free from the snares of the devil. By way of powers and principalities, torment, WITCHCRAFT possessions, of evil spirits. I've come to set the captives free from self-inflictions, and generational curses, break free before it's too late. God is the source and the strength to endure every difficult, test, trial, and tribulation this world throws at you. Don't give up, keep pushing your way the best you can keeping your heart, and hands clean. Remaining in self-control, kindness, love, longsuffering, patience, gentleness, goodness, faith, meekness, temperance, and humbleness.

I pray it's something in this book to help inspire and encourage all who reads it. No one's life is the same, but we will have to stand up and face many things in life we didn't sign up for. Put all your cares and concerns in the hand of God, by praying and making your request known unto God. then having faith that whatsoever you have prayed for God will grant it if it's in his will for your life. No matter how hard life gets don't stop believing in God.

Do good over evil. Don't look for rewards from people after doing good for people, know that our Father in heaven is the reward at the end of days. Read your word of God daily to help you keep your faith and strength when being tried and tested.

The word of God is a deliverer in of itself. As he made ways, and escapes in the biblical days he will also be a protection, and guidance in your days. Your faith is the key, never let it go. God bless you all thank you for taking your time to read my story of many trials and tribulations. May this book be your strength to remind you that no matter what the case may be, may God deliver you from it all. Let God arise and let his enemies be scattered the blood hallelujah, and Jesus May the love of God and the sweet fellowship of the Holy Spirit be with you now and forever, in Jesus Christ name Amen.

I love you with the love of God. Stay balanced mentally, physically, spiritually, emotionally, and financially. Let God have total control of your life; you won't go wrong. Be prepared to walk with your God all alone once you really give your mind, body and soul to God the enemy will use the closest ones you love against you. He will turn all against you if he can be careful of people. Only trust God. Anybody can switch up on you and betray you in seconds. Expect new beginnings to show up in your life. God is a promise keeper, what he did for me he will do for you. If you only hold to your faith in God. Daily command your flesh to decrease and allow the Holy Spirit to increase. It's much needed in the fresh start of a new day, the whole armor of God. Ephesians 6:10-24 "put on so that you're walking in the spirit and not in the flesh." Let God into your heart, it's the best thing you can do in your life. If you have never accepted God, and his son Jesus Christ, you still have time to do so by confessing out of your mouth Romans 10:9, and believing he died and rose on the third day with all power in his hands. Jesus Christ died for all our sins. Bare and carry your cross whatever God requires of you, be obedient, and you will forever be protected from the wiles of the devil. When temptations come God will raise up a standard against the enemy.

Don't forget to have charity when it is needed. This could be your time, talent, money, love, prayers, and energy. Only what you do for Christ will last. Stay focused on the salvation of Jesus Christ, when GOD corrects, rebukes, chastises and reproofs you it's out of his love for you as his child, take the discipline, and change from your sinful ways be born again, and baptized by water and the Holy Spirit. Walk away from the sin, close the door, and be Holy as he is Holy. Be thankful for the scars, pains, and rejections. It's all to build you up to be the person God can use for his glory. No man or woman will receive God's glory. You will overcome the challenges of life, by the words of your testimonies. God will not put on you more than you can bear. Remember to think positivity and speak positive. It will make a difference in your circumstances. THIS IS HOW I MADE IT THROUGH THE FIRE WITHOUT A BURN ON ME, I'M A SURVIVOR HOW I MADE IT!

THE END ……

Made in the USA
Columbia, SC
15 June 2023